Operations Management Demystified

A Springboard for Further Study

Jitendra.M.Pant

Dedicated to my parents
Late Shri Lalit Mohan Pant and
Late Smt Mohini Pant.

And to my eldest brother
Late Shri Krishna Mohan Pant.

Table Of Contents

Acknowledgement

Writing "Operations Management Demystified: A Springboard for Further Study" has been a deeply rewarding journey, and it would not have been possible without the support, guidance, and encouragement of many individuals.

First and foremost, I would like to express my deepest gratitude to my family. To my wife, Sunita, whose unwavering support and patience have been my anchor; to my children Kushagra and Prerna, and their spouse Shilpa and Paritosh, whose encouragement and understanding have always inspired me to pursue my passions. Not to forget my lovely grandchildren Siddharth and Khushi, whose smile and sweet talk full of questions which I am mostly not able to answer, drives me to write with the belief that they will read my book some day and remember me fondly.

I am profoundly grateful to my teachers and mentors from the Indian Institute of Technology, Delhi. The rigorous academic environment and the wealth of knowledge imparted there laid the foundation for my career and shaped my understanding of engineering and operations management.

A heartfelt thanks to my colleagues and friends in the industry. Your insights, collaboration, and shared experiences have enriched my professional journey. Specifically, I would like to acknowledge the teams at Larsen & Toubro Ltd, Sunflag Iron and Steel, Orient Bell Ltd, Khandelwal Cables Ltd, Shree Cement Ltd, BEC Fertilisers, BEC Engineering, Wolkem Ltd, Macrographics Ltd, Motherson Sumi Systems Ltd, Doshi Ion and Chemicals Ltd, GAIL, Sunflag Textile & Knitwear Mills Ltd, Jayaswals Neco Group, Hindustan Unilever, Tata Motors, NTPC, Maruti, Dabur, Mafatlal Textiles, Escorts, Hero Honda, Bajaj Auto, JK Tyres, Chambal Fertilisers, Adani Ports and SEZ, THDC, and many others. Your dedication to excellence in operations has been a source of inspiration and learning for me.

I would like to extend my appreciation to the numerous individuals who have contributed to this book through their expertise and feedback. Special thanks to ChatGPT for the editorial support and for being a handy resource. Many thanks to Adobe for the AI tool of text to images, few of those images have been used here.

A special mention of appreciation to the management institutes, namely Amity Business School, EMPI Business School, BIMTECH in initial stages when it was in Delhi, Apeejay, Hamdard, NIESBUD, Aravali Institute of management and few others, where I taught Operations management as a Visiting Professor, and to the student learners who sought to understand the intricacies of operations management. All of them are now in senior positions in industry and are in touch with me for mentoring and coaching sessions on Operation management which gives me immense satisfaction. Your curiosity and quest for knowledge have motivated me to share my experiences and insights. It is my hope that this book serves as a useful resource and a source of inspiration for you.

I have shared many of my power point slides used during my presentations on Operations Management as a memoir of those days, and I am thankful to all those who gave me that opportunity.

To all who have been part of this journey, whether directly or indirectly, my heartfelt thanks. This book is a reflection of our collective experiences, and I am grateful to have had the fortune to learn and grow alongside such remarkable individuals.

21 July 2024 Jitendra. M. Pant
New Delhi

Preface

Though many economists disagree, I have always believed that India should dominate manufacturing. This would not only increase our GDP and self-sufficiency but also provide gainful employment at different skill levels. Like China, we too can become a manufacturing hub, producing quality and value-added products. By moving men and women from agriculture to the manufacturing workforce with focused training, we can significantly improve their earnings. Currently, the strain on farmers with fractured land holdings drives many to despair, even to the point of suicide.

My book, "Operations Management Demystified: A Springboard for Further Study" , is not a textbook in the traditional sense. Those are already available for rigorous study by students and professionals. Instead, this book aims to whet the readers' appetites, to spark curiosity and excitement about operations management—a field that pervades our homes, shops, services, and manufacturing units of all sizes. If successful, this book will help demystify the often opaque world of operations and encourage people from diverse educational backgrounds to confidently engage in this vital area.

As an engineer from the Indian Institute of Technology, Delhi, with over four decades of experience in the industry—both as a full-time professional and a consultant—I have had the opportunity to learn operations from input to output across a range of industries. These include steel, automobiles, textiles, tiles, fertilizers, engineering, electrical switchgear, wires and cables, bulbs, soap making, picture tubes, electronics, food processing, mineral processing, modern ports and SEZs, technology-based warehousing, and the service industry.

I would like to highlight some of the industries where I learned various facets of operations management from start to finish:

- Larsen & Toubro Ltd, Mumbai: Fabrication and machine shop plant manufacturing light, medium, and heavy equipment, including nuclear reactors, pressure vessels, and heat exchangers.

-Sunflag Iron and Steel, Bhandara: A large integrated steel plant producing special steel for automobiles, railways, and defense.

-Orient Bell Ltd: Tile manufacturing plants in Sikandrabad (U.P.), Hoskote (Bengaluru), and Dora (Gujarat).

-Khandelwal Cables Ltd, Vadodara: Manufacturing electrical wires and cables.

-Shree Cement Ltd, Beawar: Cement manufacturing.

-BEC Fertilisers: Fertilizer and acid manufacturing plants in Jhagadia (Gujarat) and Bilaspur (Chhattisgarh).

-BEC Engineering, Bhilai: Fabrication and machine shop plant for Railways and other sectors.

-Wolkem Ltd, Udaipur: Mineral processing plant.

-Macrographics Ltd, Delhi: Service industry in graphic design, content creation, and printing.

-Motherson Sumi Systems Ltd, Noida, Gurgaon: Manufacturing wiring harnesses primarily for automobiles.

-Doshi Ion and Chemicals Ltd, Ahmedabad: Water treatment solutions—manufacturing and service.

-GAIL, Vijaipur: Gas plant(natural, LPG) near Guna, Madhya Pradesh.

-Sunflag Textile & Knitwear Mills Ltd, Nairobi: Manufacturing spinning, woven fabrics, knitted fabrics, and garments.

-Jayaswals Neco Group, Raipur: Pig iron plant, steel plant, various castings, ferro alloys, infrastructure, and mining projects.

-Hindustan Unilever: Detergent soap manufacturing plants in Orai (U.P.) and Chindwara (M.P.).

-Tata Motors, Lucknow: Truck manufacturing plant.

-NTPC: Power plants in Dadri, Faridabad, Korba, Ramagundam, Singrauli, Tanda, and Bongaigaon.

-Maruti: Car manufacturing plant in Gurgaon and Maruti automobile ancillaries.

- Dabur: Manufacturing plants in Sahibabad and Alwar for Ayurvedic healthcare products.

-Mafatlal Textiles, Nadiad: Textile manufacturing in Gujarat.

- Escorts, Hero Honda, Bajaj Auto: Two-wheeler and tractor manufacturing plants at

Faridabad, Gurgaon and Aurangabad respectively.

- JK Tyres, Kankroli: Tyre manufacturing in Rajasthan.

-Chambal Fertilisers, Kota: Urea and chemical manufacturing.

-Adani Ports and SEZ, Mundra; Modern warehousing and logistics at Moga; Adani Agrifresh state of srt warehouse for apples in Himachal Pradesh..

-THDC, Tehri: Hydroelectric power plant and dam in Garhwal.

-Others: Switchgear and Lamps Manufacturing at Noida; colour picture tubes manufacturing with Japanese collaboration (Toshiba and Mitsubishi) at Sahibababd; Shot blasting machines manufacturing in Jodhpur.

In this book, I share my experiences in operations management, aligning them with what is taught in formal engineering and management schools, combined with insights from various training programs that employers may offer for skill upgrades—programs that employees often attend grudgingly and learn little from.

Few of the slides used in my speaking sessions on Operations Management in industry and management institutes have been provided in the end as an Appendix. Some of my students and participants in training sessions, who are now in senior positions, wanted this inclusion so that they could use it on occasions.

The slides for me were a reference and an outline to follow lest I drift which some may call as 'scope creep'.

If this book inspires even one person to delve deeper into operations management, my efforts will be gratified.

Happy reading!

Jitendra M. Pant
21 July 2024
New Delhi

1
Introduction to Operations Management

Operations management is the strategic function within an organization responsible for overseeing the production of goods and services. It encompasses the planning, organizing, and controlling of resources and processes to ensure efficient and effective operations.

The operations system serves as the core component of an organization, embodying the processes, people, technology, and resources dedicated to transforming inputs into valuable outputs. It encompasses everything from manufacturing facilities and supply chains to service delivery networks and customer support operations.

In essence, the operations system is the backbone of an organization, playing a pivotal role in fulfilling customer demands, optimizing resource utilization, and driving organizational success. It involves the coordination of various functions and departments to achieve operational excellence, streamline processes, and maximize productivity.

The Operation system is a closed loop system with well-defined deliverables which are met through a value adding conversion process using the inputs of the typical 4Ms of Man, Material, Machine and Method. To these 4Ms, two more namely Measurement and Money have to be added to make it pragmatic and relevant. The Ms are as mnemonic, Man stands

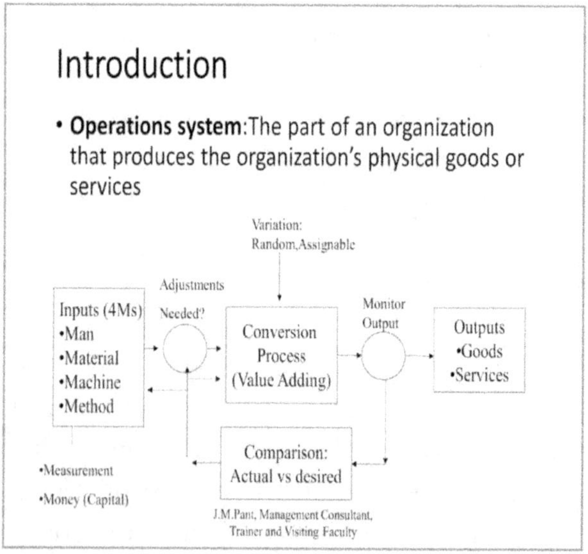
Introduction
• Operations system:The part of an organization that produces the organization's physical goods or services
Variation:
Random,Assignable
Adjustments
Needed?
Inputs (4Ms)
•Man
•Material
•Machine
•Method
Conversion
Process
(Value Adding)
Monitor
Output
Outputs
•Goods
•Services
Comparison:
Actual vs desired
•Measurement
•Money (Capital)
J.M.Pant, Management Consultant,
Trainer and Visiting Faculty

for People, Method includes Process and System, Machine is for Equipment, and Money implies Capital.

The output of goods and services is measured not only in quantity, productivity and quality, but also safety, delivery, cost and morale or what is universally understood as P, Q, C, D, S, M.

Variation is intrinsic to process and cause can be assignable or random. The output is monitored with reference to target and adjustments made in inputs and process to meet the targeted standard.

In this dynamic and increasingly competitive business landscape, effective operations management is essential for organizations to remain agile, responsive, and profitable. By continuously improving processes, leveraging technology, and aligning operations with strategic objectives, businesses can enhance efficiency, reduce costs, and deliver exceptional value to customers.

2
Historical Development

Frederick Taylor and Scientific Management (Late 19th to Early 20th Century)

1. Frederick Taylor is often regarded as the father of scientific management.
2. Taylor's work focused on applying scientific principles to management practices, aiming to optimize productivity and efficiency in industrial settings.
3. He introduced methods such as time and motion studies to analyze and streamline work processes.
4. Taylor's ideas laid the foundation for modern operations management by emphasizing systematic approaches to improving efficiency.

Charles Babbage and the Origins of Operations Research (19th Century)

1. Charles Babbage, a mathematician and engineer, made significant contributions to the field of operations management through his work on the principles of industrial engineering.

2. Babbage's concept of the "division of labour" and his analytical engines laid the groundwork for modern computational and management techniques.

Toyota Production System (TPS) and Lean Manufacturing (20th Century)

1. The Toyota Production System (TPS), developed by Toyota in the 20th century, revolutionized manufacturing processes.
2. TPS emphasized principles such as Just-In-Time production, continuous improvement (Kaizen), and respect for people.
3. Taiichi Ohno and Shigeo Shingo are often credited with the development and implementation of TPS.
4. TPS became the foundation for lean manufacturing practices adopted by companies worldwide, focusing on eliminating waste and maximizing value for customers.

W.Edwards Deming and Total Quality Management (TQM) (20th Century)

1. W.Edwards Deming, an American statistician and management consultant, played a pivotal role in

promoting quality management principles.

2. Deming's ideas, often associated with Total Quality Management (TQM), emphasized the importance of statistical process control, continuous improvement, and customer focus. His teachings revolutionised Japanese industry after World War II and influenced quality practices globally.
3. Deming's famous "14 Points" provided a framework to achieve quality and operational excellence.

Contemporary Trends and Developments (21st Century)

In the 21st century, operations management has evolved to incorporate digital technologies, automation, and data analytics.

1. Concepts such as Industry 4.0, which integrates cyber-physical systems and the Internet of Things (IoT), are shaping modern manufacturing and service industries. AI and Machine learning, robots and automation, and fully automatic plants with no or few humans totally run by technology will become quite common.

2. Agile methodologies, originally developed in software development, are increasingly being applied to operations management to enhance flexibility and responsiveness.
3. Quality standards are being raised. We no longer talk about defects in percentage but in ppm levels with purchase orders, for example, specifying acceptable quality level as 230 ppm, while the aim is to achieve six sigma and beyond in manufacturing and services, which is 3.4 defects in a million close to zero defects.
4. Sustainability and ethical considerations are gaining prominence, leading to the adoption of environmentally friendly practices and socially responsible supply chains. For example, manufacturing of green hydrogen from process of electrolysis driven by renewable energy like solar, wind and hydel, and making of steel using green hydrogen as reducing agent in place of coke . Such plants are in plan in India with front runners being Adani, L&T, Tatas, and Reliance.

3
Operations Pyramid

The goal of a business organisation is to earn money, that is profits, while that of non-profitable organisations like NGOs would be to generate surplus to fuel their mission.

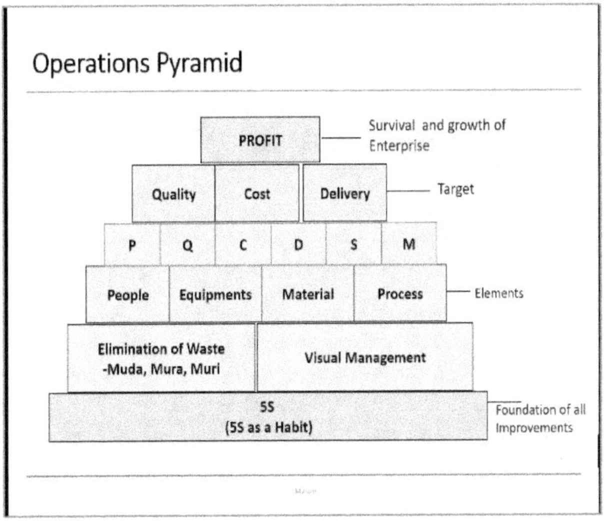

Operations Pyramid
PROFIT
Survival and growth of Enterprise
Quality
Cost
Delivery
Target
P
Q
C
D
S
M
People
Equipments
Material
Process
Elements
Elimination of Waste -Muda, Mura, Muri
Visual Management
5S (5S as a Habit)
Foundation of all Improvements

The three main targets from Operations contribution to profits would be Quality, Cost and Delivery: the subset being Productivity, Quality, Cost, Delivery, Safety and Morale-PQCDSM. which would be possible by using the elements of People, Equipment, Materials and Process through continuous Elimination of Waste and Visual Management. The nuances of Waste are best described though the three Japanese words Muda, Mura and Muri.

The foundation of improvements and operations excellence is 5S, which should be practised daily and as a habit.

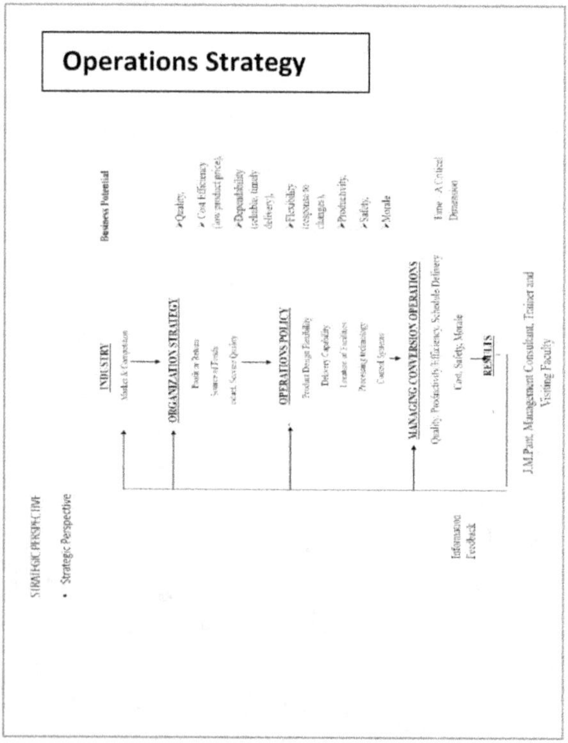

Operations Strategy
Strategic Perspective
Business Potential
INDUSTRY
ORGANIZATION STRATEGY
OPERATIONS POLICY
MANAGING CONVERSION OPERATIONS
RESULTS

4
Efficient and Effective

The terms "efficient" and "effective" are often used interchangeably, but they have distinct meanings:

1. **Efficient**

- Efficiency refers to the ability to accomplish a task or achieve a goal with the least amount of wasted time, effort, or resources.
- It focuses on maximizing productivity and minimizing waste.
- An efficient process or system produces the desired results using the fewest inputs or resources possible.
- For example, an efficient manufacturing process would produce a high volume of products using minimal raw materials, labour, and time.

2. **Effective**

- Effectiveness, on the other hand, refers to the ability to achieve the desired outcome or result.
- It focuses on accomplishing goals or objectives and meeting expectations.

- An effective process or system achieves its intended purpose and delivers the desired outcomes.

- For example, an effective marketing campaign would successfully reach and persuade its target audience, leading to increased sales or brand awareness.

In summary:

- Efficiency is about doing things right, focusing on optimizing processes and resource utilization.
- Effectiveness is about doing the right things, focusing on achieving desired outcomes and fulfilling objectives.

While efficiency and effectiveness are related concepts, they are not synonymous. A process can be efficient but not effective if it fails to achieve its intended goals, and vice versa. However, organizations strive to be both efficient and effective in order to maximize performance and achieve success.

5
Productivity

Productivity refers to the efficiency with which resources are utilized to produce goods and services. There are different ways to measure productivity, including total productivity and factor productivity:

1. Total Productivity (TP)

- Total productivity measures the efficiency of all inputs (e.g., labour, capital, materials) used in the production process relative to the total output produced.
- It provides an overall assessment of the effectiveness of resource utilization in generating output.
- Total productivity is calculated as the ratio of total output to total input. The formula for total productivity is:

Total Productivity=Total Output/ Total Input

2. Factor Productivity (FP)

- Factor productivity focuses on the efficiency of specific factors of production, such as labour, capital, or materials, relative to the output produced.

- It allows for a more detailed analysis of the contribution of individual factors to overall productivity.
- Factor productivity is calculated as the ratio of output to a specific input factor. The formula for factor productivity depends on the input being analysed. For example:

Labor Productivity= Output / Labor Input
Capital Productivity=Output/Capital Input
Material Productivity=Output/ Material Input

Both total productivity and factor productivity are important metrics for evaluating and improving operational efficiency. Total productivity provides a comprehensive view of overall efficiency, while factor productivity allows for a more nuanced analysis of the contribution of specific inputs to overall output. By measuring and analysing productivity at both levels, organizations can identify opportunities for optimization and improvement in their production processes.

Exercise

- The manager of a cola bottling plant came to work early on Friday, and checked labor efficiency figures:
- Mon 102%
- Tue 94%
- Wed 87%
- Thurs 96 man hours worked and bottled 1025
- cases.
- Standard labor output is 12.5 cases per man hour. Plot daily efficiency and comment on the productivity values with likely reasons for high/low productivity.

Exercise

- For a 12 month period last year, ABC restaurant averaged 224 customers served each day: Hours are 8a.m to 11p.m spread over two shifts, and 6 employees make up the total staff with 3 persons in each shift.Performance has been as under:

	Customers	Strength
Mon	264	6 regular
Tue	232	4 people full time + 2 persons for 4 hours each
Wed	220	6 regular + 2 casual
Thurs	200	6 regular
Fri	180	5 regular (1 absent).

- Will the result please the owner? What is the trend of labor productivity? Likely reasons for low productivity?

J.M Pant, Management Consultant, Trainer and Visiting Faculty

6
Quality Concept

Quality is external and internal customer satisfaction.

Quality is fitness for use.

Quality is making what the customer wants so as to delight the customer.

It means near 100% accuracy in the first run.
First time right and Quality first attitude.

Quality is meeting standards.

Quality implies No rework

Quality means No complaints or reprocessing requirement from the customer

Quality is pursuing what is ideal. Not making any compromises.

Two components of Quality:

Product features and ***freedom from deficiencies*** are the main determinants of customer satisfaction.

Product Features

- Performance
- Reliability
- Durability
- Ease of use
- Serviceability
- Aesthetics
- Availability of options and expandability
- Reputation

Freedom from deficiencies.

- Product free of defects and errors at delivery, during use and during servicing.
- Sales, billing and other business processes free of errors.

Freedom from deficiencies refers to quality of conformance. Increasing the quality of conformance results in lower costs, fewer complaints and increased customer satisfaction.

7
Relationship of Quality, Cost and Productivity

The relationship between quality, cost, and productivity is fundamental in operations management and organizational performance. Here's how these elements are interconnected:

1. Quality

- Quality refers to the level of excellence or superiority of a product or service. It encompasses attributes such as reliability, durability, performance, and customer satisfaction.
- High-quality products or services meet or exceed customer expectations, leading to increased customer loyalty, positive brand reputation, and competitive advantage.
- Ensuring high quality often involves investing in processes, materials, and skilled labour to meet quality standards and specifications.

2. Cost

- Cost refers to the expenses incurred in the production of goods or delivery of services. It includes direct costs (e.g., materials, labour) and indirect costs (e.g., overhead, administrative expenses).

- Managing costs is essential for profitability and sustainability. Organizations strive to minimize costs while maintaining quality to maximize profitability and remain competitive in the market.

- Poor quality can result in increased costs due to rework, scrap, warranty claims, and customer dissatisfaction. Conversely, investing in quality upfront can lead to cost savings over the long term by reducing defects and waste.

Cost of Poor Quality

Poor quality results in internal failures when quality checks are done and rejections because of defects at receipt stage of incoming material or defects produced at source of creating product or service are identified. Sometimes defects can be salvaged through rework at receipt stage, at source or in line of production. Both defects and rework result in opportunity cost and loss of contribution through lost Production.

If poor quality is not detected in plant and product goes to market where it fails, there will be a big cost not only due to warranty claims, customer returns and frequent meetings and travel to salvage position with the customer, but a likely drop in market share, good will and brand image due to adverse word of mouth publicity and customer dissatisfaction. If negotiation results in selling the product at reduced price, there is cost of reduction in value because of downgraded products or services.
If yields are poor and rejections high, planners will provide for excess material consumption provision in MRP due to inadequate process increasing cost further.

As Philip Crosby had said 'quality is free' as the cost goes up several times due to poor quality, sometimes 30 to 40% of cost of sales.

3. Productivity

- Productivity measures the efficiency of production processes in terms of output per unit of input (e.g., labor, capital, time).
- Improving productivity involves maximizing output while minimizing input or

resource utilisation. It leads to increased efficiency, higher output levels, and lower costs per unit produced.

- Quality can influence productivity positively by reducing defects, rework, and waste, thus improving process efficiency and throughput.
- Conversely, sacrificing quality to boost productivity can lead to increased costs associated with defects, rework, and customer dissatisfaction, undermining overall efficiency and profitability.

The common myth is that if Quality goes up. Productivity will reduce and cost will go up.

Reality is the opposite for if Quality improves, waste is reduced and cost comes down, yields improve and productivity increases.

Productivity goes down when Quality improvement is planned through 100% inspection and screening of good and bad items.

When Quality is built in the process itself, it results in productivity improvement.

It is meaningless to raise productivity when defective products are being produced.

When Quality improves, Productivity improves because Waste is eliminated. Waste here means anything which does not add value to the product and service.

The rider is: **Capability must exist**. A capable typist can type 40 words a minute without a mistake, while an untrained typist will make mistakes at this speed and rework, or slow down speed for error free typing in which case productivity falls.

Capability is of Process, Equipment, and People.

In summary, the relationship between quality, cost, and productivity is symbiotic:
- High-quality products and services contribute to customer satisfaction, brand loyalty, and competitive advantage.
- Managing costs effectively while maintaining quality is crucial for profitability and sustainability.

- Improving productivity through efficient processes and resource utilisation can enhance competitiveness and profitability, but it should not come at the expense of quality. Balancing these factors is essential for achieving optimal operational performance and organizational success.

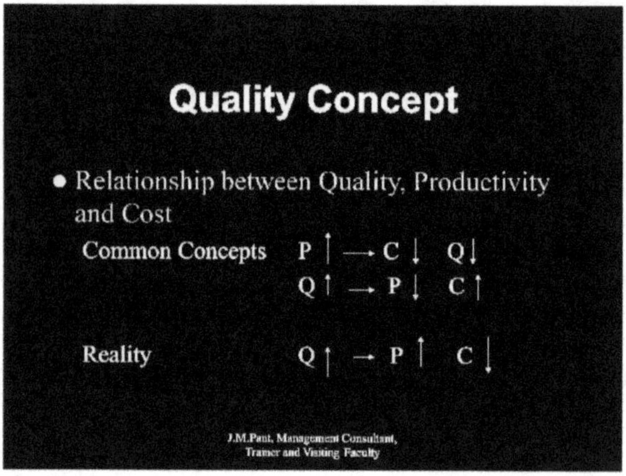
Quality Concept
• Relationship between Quality, Productivity and Cost
Common Concepts
P ↑ → C ↓ Q↓
Q ↑ → P ↓ C ↑
Reality
Q ↑ → P ↑ C ↓
J.M.Pant, Management Consultant, Trainer and Visiting Faculty

8
Factors of Poor Quality

Internal failures and external failures are two categories of factors that contribute to poor quality in products or services:

1. Internal Failures

- Internal failures occur within the organization's control and are typically detected before products or services reach customers.
- These failures often arise during the production process or while the product is still within the organization's facilities. They can also occur at the receipt stage of materials or at source of procurement materials, and even during transport.
- Common examples of internal failures include:
    - Defective components or materials: Flaws or defects in raw materials, parts, or components used in the production process can lead to internal failures.
    - Equipment malfunctions: Issues with machinery, tools, or equipment can result in

manufacturing defects or errors during production.

- Poor workmanship: Errors or mistakes made by workers during assembly, fabrication, or installation processes can result in internal failures.

- Inadequate quality control: Insufficient quality control measures or ineffective inspection processes may fail to detect defects or deviations from quality standards, allowing defective products to pass through.

- Internal failures incur costs for rework at source, receipt stores or in processing line, scrap, and repairs, as well as damage to the organization's reputation and customer satisfaction if not addressed promptly.

Rework is lost contribution through loss of production. One may sell goods at a discount to recover some money but that comes at huge cost to brand, customer goodwill and loss of customer satisfaction resulting in loss of market share. The image of producer gets cast as a producer of shoddy and inferior goods and services.

2. External Failures

- External failures occur after products or services have been delivered to customers and are detected outside the organization.
- These failures often result from defects or deficiencies that were not identified or addressed before the product reached the customer.
- Common examples of external failures include:
  - Product recalls: Recalls occur when products are found to have defects or safety issues that pose risks to consumers, prompting the manufacturer to withdraw the product from the market.
  - Customer complaints: Complaints from customers regarding product defects, malfunctions, or poor performance indicate external failures.
  - Warranty claims: Customers may submit warranty claims for repairs or replacements due to defects or failures in products they have purchased.
  - Returns and refunds: Customers returning products for refunds or exchanges due to quality issues represent external failures.

- External failures can result in significant costs for the organization, including field visits, meetings with customer, negotiation and discounts, warranty expenses, legal liabilities, brand damage, and loss of customer trust and loyalty.

In summary, internal failures occur within the organization's control and are typically detected before products reach customers, while external failures occur after delivery and are detected by customers or other external stakeholders. Both types of failures can have adverse effects on quality, customer satisfaction, and the organization's reputation and financial performance. Therefore, effective quality management practices are essential to identify, prevent, and address both internal and external failures to ensure product quality and customer satisfaction.

9
Muda, Mura, Muri

Why is the productivity low even when people are working very hard? Is it because of lax supervision or are there some hidden reasons?

Productivity is reduced because of wasteful actions which act as a drag.

Japanese call them the three Ms-Muda, Mura, Muri-which express three nuances of Waste.
Muda forms seven types of Waste, and is reactive approach.
Mura is variation, unevenness, inconsistency, and waste linked to it.
Muri is strain, excess work beyond capacity, overloading, and waste attributed to it.
Mura and Muri are proactive approaches to be taken care of during design, planning and policy making stage.

These bugs have to be eliminated or minimised. With them around, productivity will fall.

Muda

1. Inventory/Storage - raw materials, components in-process, finished goods.
2. Defects, rework, spoilage, deterioration, warranty claims, customer returns.
3. Waiting, Idling-breakdowns, process problems, set up and change over time, no utility, no sale plan, idling manpower.
4. Unnecessary Transportation-within plant, in- bound and outbound logistics. Bad plant layout and incorrect choice of material handling system.
5. Over-production; producing more than demand.
6. Unnecessary motion-bad design of work place or positioning of switches etc causing extra motion of hand, arms, foot etc.
7. Unnecessary processing-bad method /process, design.

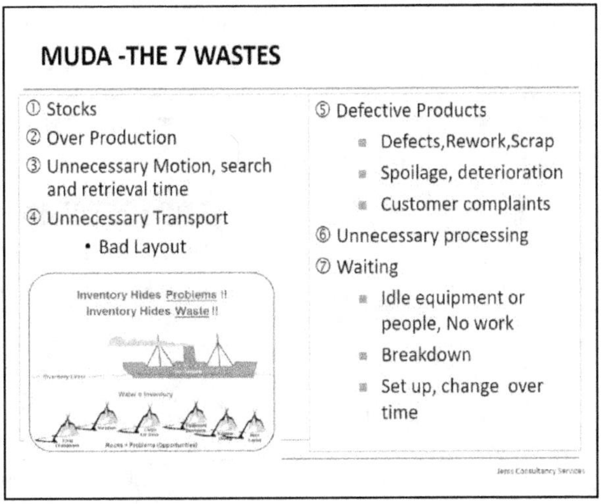
MUDA -THE 7 WASTES
① Stocks
② Over Production
③ Unnecessary Motion, search and retrieval time
④ Unnecessary Transport
• Bad Layout
Inventory Hides Problems !!
Inventory Hides Waste !!
⑤ Defective Products
Defects,Rework,Scrap
Spoilage, deterioration
Customer complaints
⑥ Unnecessary processing
⑦ Waiting
Idle equipment or people, No work
Breakdown
Set up, change over time

Mura

Waste because of unstable process, excess variation in quality, production jerks, sometimes less or no production and sometimes high requirement, irregular use of person and equipment/machine. This unevenness throws planning haywire and confuses people lowering productivity.

Muri

Waste because of strain and overloading beyond capacity of people, facilities, transport, conveyors, containers, racks etc.

If operations continue like this for long, there will be operational failures, accidents, absenteeism, and productivity will sharply decline.

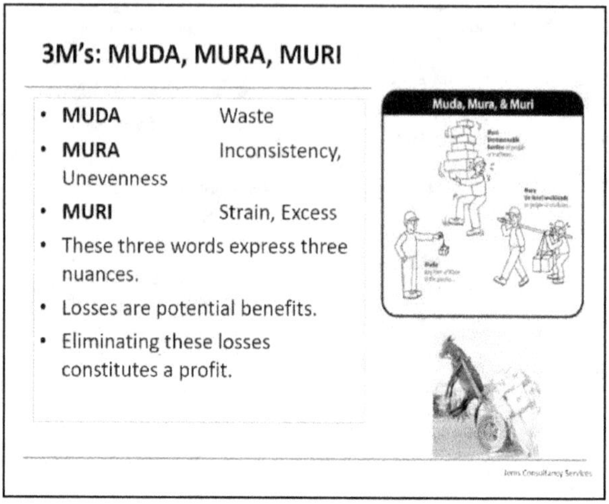
3M's: MUDA, MURA, MURI
• MUDA Waste
• MURA Inconsistency, Unevenness
• MURI Strain, Excess
• These three words express three nuances.
• Losses are potential benefits.
• Eliminating these losses constitutes a profit.
Muda, Mura, & Muri

The SEVEN WASTES
Motion
Defects / Rejects / Re-work
Over - Production
Storage / Inventory
Transportation
Over - Processing
How do you spell that?
Waiting

10
Visual Management

Visual Management is by eyes. It highlights the abnormal condition and brings clarity and transparency. It allows you to see the "normal" state (standard) and allows you to quickly see a "deviation" from the standard.

Visual management provides a clear and common understanding of goals and measures. It allows people to align their actions and decisions with the overall strategic direction of the company.

It is also an open window to factory performance, and it provides the same unbiased information to everyone, whether owner, manager, operator, or visitor.

Visual management provides real-time information and feedback regarding the status of the plant.

125

Implementing Visual Management

Step 1: Decide what needs to be made visual.

<Examples>

Production targets and achievement.

Productivity levels.

Premium yields.

Equipment availability.

Safety.

Best performance, best practices.

Step 2: Set up a trigger system

Step 3: Set up a standard for action

GOAL
5318
ACTUAL
5362

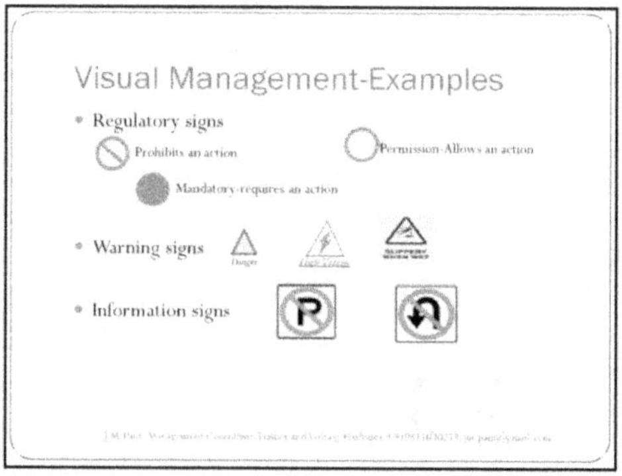
Visual Management-Examples
Regulatory signs
Prohibits an action
Permission-Allows an action
Mandatory-requires an action
Warning signs
Danger
Information signs
P

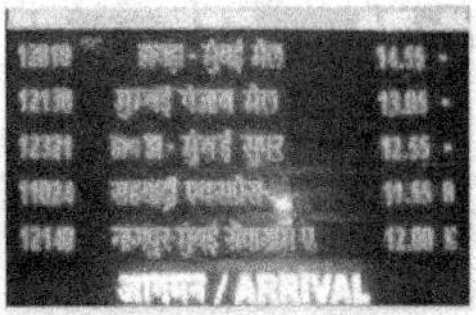

आगमन / ARRIVAL

NO
STORAGE
ALLOWED

Benefits of Visual management

- Makes work easier.
- New employees can figure out what is going on quickly.
- Problems are elevated to support staff faster.
- Identifies where things must go
- Identifies the standard quantity
- Identifies the minimum and/or maximum
- Allows us to see when the process is not working the way it should.
- Gives us a reason to ask "why."
- Often provides the trigger that something is abnormal.

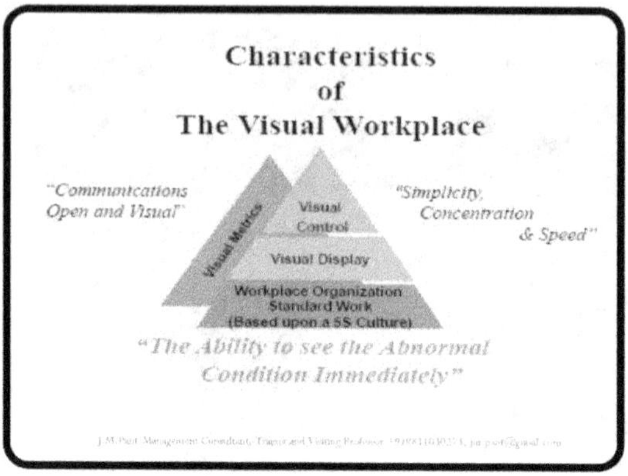
Characteristics
of
The Visual Workplace
"Communications
Open and Visual"
"Simplicity,
Concentration
& Speed"
Visual Metrics
Visual
Control
Visual Display
Workplace Organization
Standard Work
(Based upon a 5S Culture)
"The Ability to see the Abnormal
Condition Immediately"

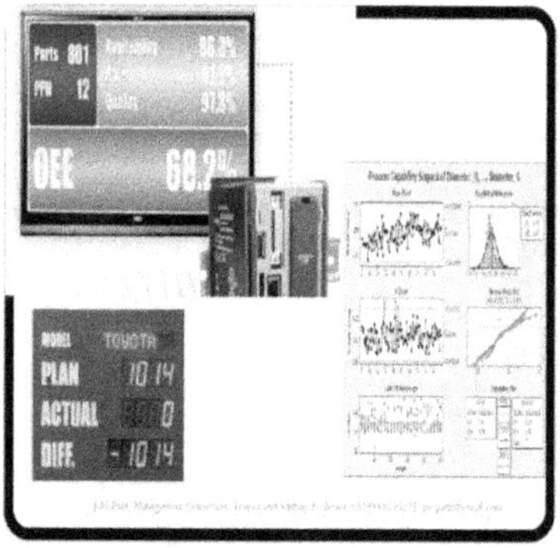
OEE
MODEL TOYOTA
PLAN 1014
ACTUAL
DIFF. -1014

11
5S

Why do we need a clean, visual plant?
A mindset which neglects a dirty and unorganised factory will never generate excellent products.
Our factory is where we all live.
Our mindset is directly reflected in our products.

5S was developed in Japan after World War II as a tool to improve quality and productivity, and make Japan competitive in the world market as exports were essential for survival of Japan. There were many contributors to development of 5S in Japan. The leading players though were Hiroyuki Hirano, Osada, and the Toyota team of father Sakichi Toyoda and son Kiichiro, and the Toyota engineer Taichi Ohno. 5S was one of the enabling techniques for the Toyota Production System or JIT as later christened by Western managers.

Sakichi Toyoda, Kiichiro and Ohno had visited U.S.A to study the production lines of Ford Motor Company and the American supermarkets. The learnings from this visit- waste in Ford's assembly line resulting in worker idling, and efficient inventory management in supermarkets of ordering based on demand- led to the development of Toyota Production System.

5S approach is a variation, an improved version, of the Western approach of housekeeping as an element of best manufacturing practices.

5S provides a structure and discipline to the improvement programs, being built of many explicit steps, each building on its predecessor.

Western management system had always emphasised on defining locations for materials and tools, and the work flow, and to this extent 5S is similar to their approach. Hirano however added a principle that items not required should be removed or stored elsewhere, thereby telling the managers to consider work flow, organising and order, and layout, only after removing the unnecessary items. Hirano taught through 5S how to reach at optimal solutions by eliminating or reducing efforts in doing non value adding work.

What is 5S?

5S is a Japanese Management approach and a commitment towards improvement of:

① **Q (Quality)** = Zero defects. Producing goods and services which satisfy customer and even delight by exceeding customer expectations.

5S helps in reducing waste in form of scrap, defectives, customer returns, leakages- water, steam, oil, air.

② **P (Productivity)** = Value Adding Output/Input

5S helps in eliminating or reducing waste, thereby reducing cost of input. With improved quality, value is added to output. Overall Productivity improves.

③ **S (Safety)**= Zero accidents

5S focuses on minor incidents like a loose nut, open wire, sparking, dust and by preventing minor incidents, major accidents are avoided.

④ **C (Cost)** = material + manpower + overheads
5S helps in saving material, man hours, energy by preventing leakages, spillages and thus reducing cost.

⑤ **D (Delivery)** = on time, speed up
5S helps in identifying points which are holding up the process, or slowing down, and through improvement in change over time, cycle time, and cutting various time losses, the overall delivery time is reduced.

⑥ **M (Morale)** = motivated and engaged people.

5S involves people though individual and group 5S activities, competitions, recognitions and awards, and brings about a quantum jump in the energy and morale of employees.

5S methodology provides importance to each employee starting from the lowest level, and fosters genuine employee pride.

5S reiterates dignity of labour, importance of process and how each job is essential to building a quality process, product and service.

5S techniques are used on a daily basis for bringing about improvements at the work place (plant and office, manufacturing and services, work and personal life).

5S are Japanese words. When written in English, the first alphabet of each word starts with a S, hence the term 5S. Their literal translation in English is difficult, but the closest meaning of each of these S is as follows.

The five S's are:

Seiri: **Sorting**, Re-Organisation
Separate and categorise into necessary & unnecessary things.
1. Remove unnecessary items
2. Classify items as per frequency of use and store them

Stop wasting time looking for things. Only keep what you need.
Reduces searching time.

Seiton : **Straighten**, Proper arrangement & maintenance, Orderliness
Location, identity, labeling, maintenance, proper storage so that necessary things may be readily available as and when required.
Thinking about how to store and keep things you need so as to guarantee Safety, Quality and Productivity.
It also enables efficient use of space. It reduces retrieval time.

Seiso : **Shine**, Cleaning
Remove dust, dirt & make things clean.
Cleaning is inspection.
Making things look new. Restoring them to their original colour.
Seiso improves Quality.

Seiketsu : **Standardise**
Develop systems, rules and procedures to maintain and monitor the first three S's. Maintain all elements of production in a clean condition.
Standardise cleanliness, lighting, colour, fonts, signage, labels, colour markings on floor, pipes, cables, structure, safety signs and so forth.

Shitsuke **: Sustain,** Discipline
Follow rules and make 5S a habit. Maintaining a stabilized workplace is an ongoing process of continuous improvement.
Proper attitude is the foundation of 5S.

Thus the 5S in English would be Sort, Straighten, Shine, Standardise, Sustain

Process of 5S

1.Record rhe situation: Before 5S and after 5S
2.Photography method: Take pictures before 5S and after 5S from the same marked spot, at the same height, same angle, so that one can compare like with like.
3.Red tag method: Red tag unwanted items and put them in Red tag store to be disposed off at a later time.

For more on 5S, read the author's book: 5S-First Vital Step towards Operations Excellence (available at pothi, amazon, flipkart)

5S-The Foundation For TPM, TQM

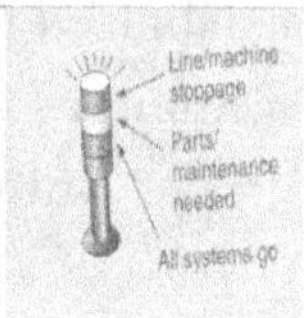
Line/machine stoppage
Parts/ maintenance needed
All systems go

Two Approaches:
Red tag method
Photography method

Reduce search and retrieval time
Keep Clean
No material in unplanned, unidentified location

Jems Consultancy Services

Bad 5S Situation

Jems Consultancy Services

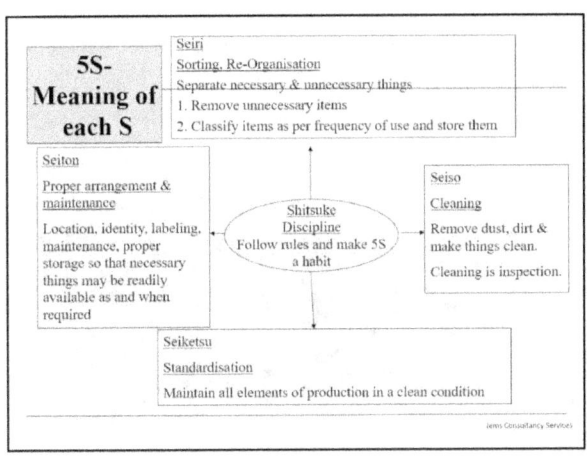

5S- Meaning of each S

Seiri

Sorting, Re-Organisation

Separate necessary & unnecessary things

1. Remove unnecessary items
2. Classify items as per frequency of use and store them

Seiton

Proper arrangement & maintenance

Location, identity, labeling, maintenance, proper storage so that necessary things may be readily available as and when required

Shitsuke

Discipline

Follow rules and make 5S a habit

Seiso

Cleaning

Remove dust, dirt & make things clean.

Cleaning is inspection.

Seiketsu

Standardisation

Maintain all elements of production in a clean condition

Jems Consultancy Services

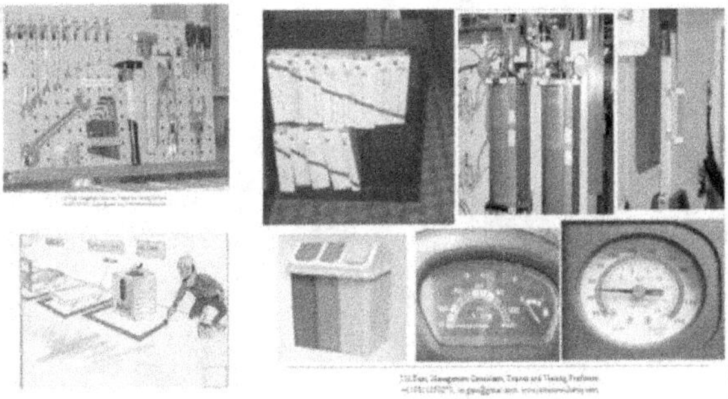

Improved 5S Situation

Jems Consultancy Services

Recording

- Photography

Before-record and storage area

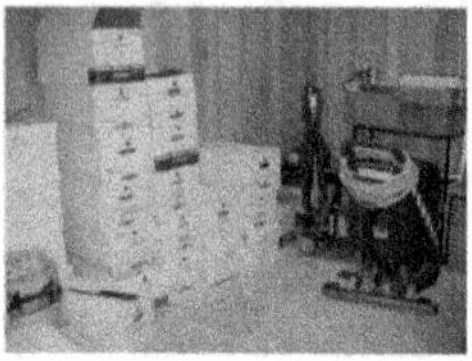

After-room available as office

Jems Consultancy Services

Seiri-scrap in different boxes

Dispose off
unnecessary items

Jems Consultancy Services

12

Design of Product and Services

In operations management, the design of products and services plays a crucial role in the overall success of an organization. It involves creating products or services that meet customer needs and expectations while optimizing resources, costs, and quality. The design process encompasses various stages, from conceptualization and development to testing, production, and delivery. Let's explore how product and service design relates to the product life cycle:

DESIGNING PRODUCTS, SERVICES AND PROCESSES

Product Life Cycle

	Start up	Rapid Growth	Maturity	Decline
Product Variety	Great →			High Standardization
Volume	Low →			High Volumes
Industry Structure	Small Competitors →			Survivors
Form of Competition	Product Characteristics	Product Quality, Availability	Price & Dependability	Price

1. Start up or Introduction Stage

- During the start-up stage of the product life cycle, the primary focus is on designing products or services that meet emerging market needs and preferences.

- Product Variety: Large
- Volume : Low
- Industry Structure: small competitors
- Form of Competition: Product Characteristics

- Design decisions made at this stage influence product features, specifications, and characteristics, setting the foundation for subsequent stages of the product life cycle.

2. Rapid Growth Stage

- As the product gains acceptance and market demand grows, operations management continues to play a vital role in product design by optimizing production processes and scaling up manufacturing capabilities.

- Product Variety: Moderate
- Volume : Moderate
- Industry Structure: more competitors

- Form of Competition: Product Quality and Availability

- Design modifications may be made to enhance product performance, improve efficiency, or introduce new features based on customer feedback and market trends.
- Operations managers collaborate with cross-functional teams to streamline production processes, reduce lead times, and enhance supply chain efficiency to meet growing demand effectively.

3. Maturity Stage

- In the maturity stage, products or services reach their peak sales levels, and competition intensifies.

- Product Variety: high standardisation
- Volume High
- Industry Structure: several competitors
- Form of Competition: Price and dependability

- Operations management focuses on optimizing product design for cost efficiency, process reliability, and quality consistency to maintain profitability in a competitive market.

- Design improvements may involve value engineering to identify cost-saving opportunities without compromising product performance or customer satisfaction.

- Additionally, operations managers may explore product line extensions, customization options, or service enhancements to differentiate offerings and prolong the product's life cycle.

4. Decline Stage

- In the decline stage, sales and market demand for the product begin to decline, often due to technological advancements, changing consumer preferences, or market saturation.

- Operations management may still play a role in product design by exploring ways to extend the product's life cycle through product redesign, repositioning, or cost reduction strategies.

- Design changes may focus on simplifying production processes, reducing manufacturing costs, or repackaging products to appeal to niche markets or new customer segments.

- Ultimately, operations managers must assess the viability of maintaining production for declining products and allocate resources accordingly to minimize losses and maximize profitability.

Throughout the product life cycle, effective

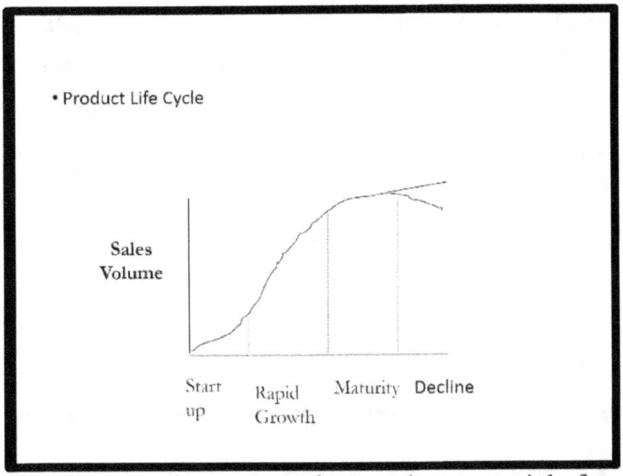
• Product Life Cycle
Sales Volume
Start up
Rapid Growth
Maturity
Decline

product and service design is essential for meeting customer needs, adapting to market dynamics, and sustaining competitive advantage. Operations management plays a central role in aligning design decisions with business objectives, optimizing production processes, and driving continuous improvement to ensure the success and longevity of products and services in the marketplace.

Research and Development

Decay curve of new product ideas.

Many ideas have to go through a screening process before one gets one good commercially viable and technically feasible product. The ideas get filtered on being impractical, lack of technology, economic analysis, and the ones which go through this lens are subjected to prototype development. Only a few pass this test, and the successful ones are thrown into market for trial run.

Perhaps one product may turn out successful during market testing.

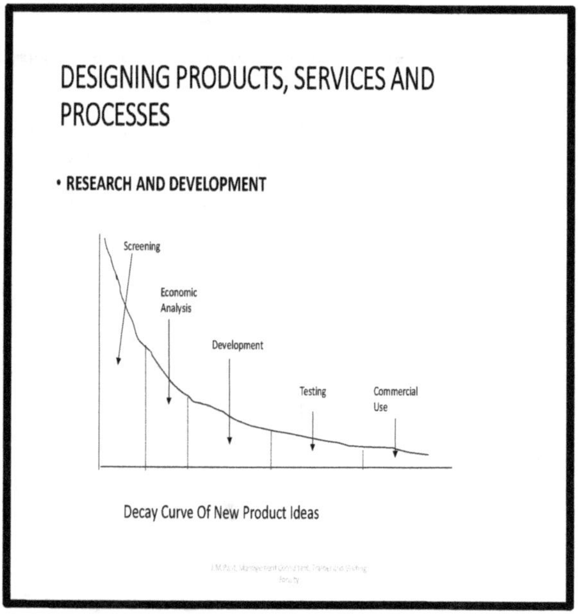
DESIGNING PRODUCTS, SERVICES AND PROCESSES
• RESEARCH AND DEVELOPMENT
Screening
Economic Analysis
Development
Testing
Commercial Use
Decay Curve Of New Product Ideas

Various types of R&D

1. Basic Research which is knowledge oriented. Research to advance the theoretical knowledge,
2. Applied Research which is research oriented to specific commercial use.
3. Development Research which converts research results into product.
4. Implementation which is building models and pilot plant for testing the product at plant or laboratory before commercial launch.

R&D could be centralised, decentralised, or a combination of the two with basic and applied research being centralised and development and implementation being decentralised.

Product Development Process

The product development process starts with identification of the needs of customer, the pains and the problem at hand, for solving which a product concept is developed which is then converted to a conceptual design. After that, detailed engineering design for product and for manufacturing is done. The product is tested and launched in market, and based on feedback further improvement on the product is done. Communication material, manuals and training is given to support the customer on product operations, installation, maintenance, and applications.

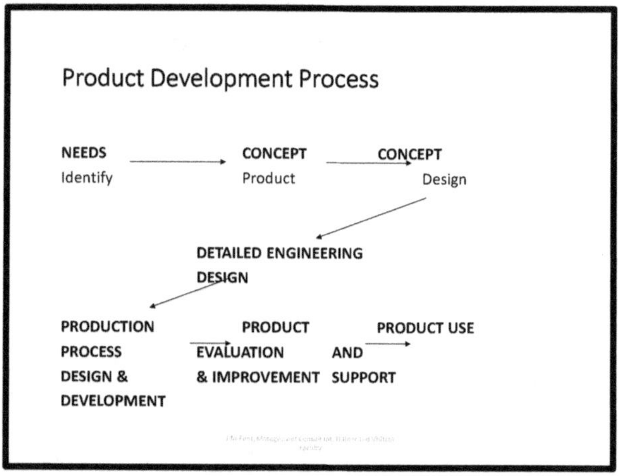

Product Development Process
NEEDS
Identify
CONCEPT
Product
CONCEPT
Design
DETAILED ENGINEERING
DESIGN
PRODUCTION
PROCESS
DESIGN &
DEVELOPMENT
PRODUCT
EVALUATION
& IMPROVEMENT
PRODUCT USE
AND
SUPPORT

Detailed engineering for product, sub-systems, components, materials, apart from dimensions, size, shape, entails:

- Design for Function
- Design for Reliability
- Design for Maintainability
- Design for Safety
- Design for Producibility – technical feasibility, cost and volumes for economic viability.

The final design output is set of drawings, manuals, documentation engineering specifications, and working prototype.

The manufacturing process design is selecting the best production process to meet the objectives, designing jigs and fixtures, tools and moulds, making standard operating processes, material planning, procurement, planning for inventory, storage, transport and distribution and developing systems for Production Planning and Control, Information Systems and HR systems.

Product Evaluation is study of field performance and feedback from failures, and to provide the R&D team with information on technical breakthroughs in materials and equipment.

It is important to educate the customer on product use and its applications to avoid early failures, and to upgrade product with design improvements. Design goal is to ensure zero or minimum warranty claims and repair service, and the organisation must have essential inventory of replacement parts, either with itself or its vendors available on demand replenishment (JIT) basis.

Modular design & Standardisation
Modular design.
Creation of products from a combination of basic, pre-existing sub systems.
For example:

- Computers configured differently through combination of RAM, disc storage, processor type and speed, monitors, keyboards, graphic and video card, sound card.
- Modular furniture which can be build through combination of basic modules; modular kitchen, and so forth.
- Car variety built on common platform.

Benefits of Modular Design

Easy to build.

Easy to maintain.

Standardisation

For example screws, bolts, motors, flanges, belts, bearings, cables, and so forth.

- No need to redesign; buy standard.
- Reduces inventory of spares.
- Reduce components production-buy standard.
- Simplify PPC, material planning.

Learning Curve

The learning curve is a graphical representation showing how the cost of producing an item decreases over time as production experience increases.

The concept was first observed by the aerospace industry in the 1930s, where it was noted that each time the cumulative production doubled, the labour hours required per unit decreased by a consistent percentage.

The Learning Curve Effect

Experience and Efficiency : As workers become more experienced with a task, they perform it more efficiently, leading to reduced time and costs.

Cumulative Production: The cumulative quantity of units produced directly influences the level of learning and efficiency gains.

Learning Rate: The rate at which learning and efficiency improvements occur is often expressed as a percentage. For example, an 80% learning rate implies that each time the cumulative production doubles, the time per unit is reduced to 80% of its previous value.

Types of Learning Curves

Linear Learning Curve: Suggests a constant rate of learning and efficiency improvement.

Logarithmic Learning Curve: Reflects a rapid initial improvement that gradually tapers off as cumulative production increases.

Exponential Learning Curve: Indicates that initial learning is slow, but once a certain level of experience is gained, efficiency improves rapidly.

Mathematical Representation

The learning curve can be represented mathematically as:

$T_n = T_1 * n^b$

where: T_n = Time taken to produce the nth unit, T_1 = Time taken to produce the first unit, n = Cumulative number of units produced and b= Learning curve exponent.

Uses of the Learning Curve in Operations Management

Cost Estimation: Helps in predicting future costs based on the expected learning and efficiency improvements. This is crucial for budgeting and financial planning.

Pricing Strategy: Businesses can set competitive prices by anticipating reduced production costs as learning progresses.

Capacity Planning: Efficiently allocating resources and planning capacity to meet future demand while considering expected improvements in productivity.

Scheduling and Lead Time: Improving scheduling accuracy and reducing lead times by accounting for efficiency gains.

Workforce Training: Identifying the need for training programs to accelerate the learning curve and enhance productivity.

Quality Improvement: As experience increases, the likelihood of errors decreases, leading to improved product quality.

Learning Curve

- **Learning Curve**

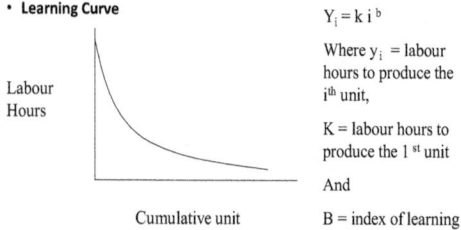

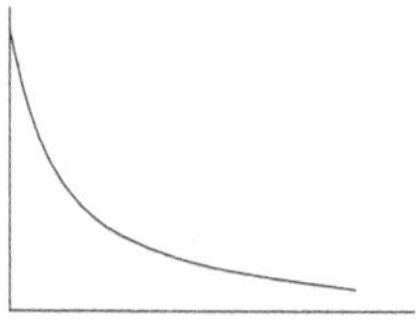
Labour Hours
Cumulative unit

$Y_i = k\, i^{b}$

Where y_i = labour hours to produce the ith unit,

K = labour hours to produce the 1st unit

And

B = index of learning

Applications:

1.Determine work force size

2.Production planning and scheduling

3.Evaluating effect of changes in tasks/ alternatives and problem solving

J.M.Pant, Management Consultant,
Trainer and Visiting Faculty

13

Reliability and Maintainability

Reliability is the probability that the product will perform as intended for prescribed lifetime under specified operating conditions.

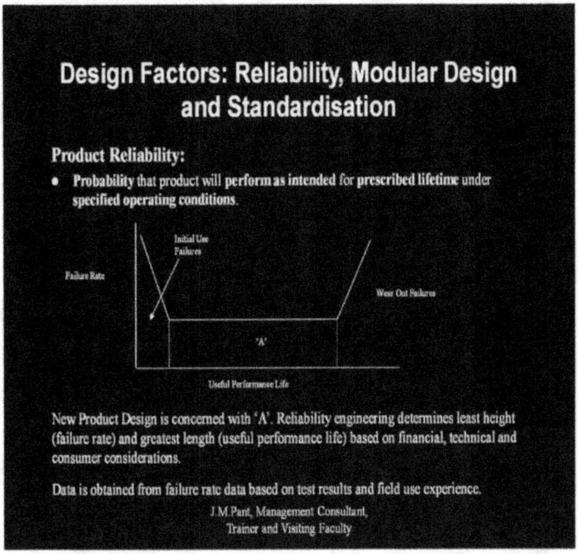

Design Factors: Reliability, Modular Design and Standardisation
Product Reliability:
• Probability that product will perform as intended for prescribed lifetime under specified operating conditions.
Initial Use Failures
Failure Rate
Wear Out Failures
'A'
Useful Performance Life
New Product Design is concerned with 'A'. Reliability engineering determines least height (failure rate) and greatest length (useful performance life) based on financial, technical and consumer considerations.
Data is obtained from failure rate data based on test results and field use experience.
J.M.Pant, Management Consultant,
Trainer and Visiting Faculty

The bath tub curve of Reliability

The bathtub curve (with failure rate in y-axis and time period in x-axis) is a graphical representation as above used in reliability engineering to illustrate the failure rate of a product over its lifetime. It resembles the shape of a bathtub, with three distinct phases: infancy or early life, useful performance life where failure is random , and old age or wear-out.

1. Early Life Phase

- The early life phase, also known as the infant mortality phase, represents the initial period after a product is put into operation.
- During this phase, the failure rate is relatively high as the product experiences failures caused by manufacturing defects, design flaws, or installation errors.
- Failures occurring in the early life phase are often attributed to "infant mortality," where weak components or improper assembly lead to premature failures.
- The goal during this phase is to identify and address these early failures through quality control measures, testing, and design improvements to prevent recurrence.

2. Useful performance life

- After the early life phase, the product enters a phase characterized by a relatively low and constant failure rate.
- During this phase, the product operates under normal conditions, and failures occur

randomly due to factors such as wear and tear, environmental stress, or chance events.

- Failures in this phase are unpredictable and may occur at any time, but they tend to be less frequent compared to the early life phase.
- Proper maintenance, regular inspections, and monitoring can help mitigate the risk of failures during this phase and extend the product's operational life.

3. Wear-Out Phase

- As the product continues to age and accumulate usage, it eventually enters the wear-out phase.
- During this phase, the failure rate begins to increase gradually as components degrade, wear out, or reach the end of their useful life.
- Failures in the wear-out phase become more frequent and predictable, leading to a higher likelihood of system breakdowns and downtime.
- The wear-out phase may be accelerated by factors such as harsh operating conditions, inadequate maintenance, or the absence of replacement parts.
- Eventually, the product reaches a point where the failure rate exceeds an acceptable

level, prompting the need for replacement, refurbishment, or retirement.

Understanding the bathtub curve of reliability is essential for product designers, manufacturers, and maintenance professionals to develop strategies for enhancing product quality, reliability, and longevity. By addressing issues related to early life failures, implementing proactive maintenance practices, and planning for end-of-life considerations, organizations can improve product performance, minimize downtime, and enhance customer satisfaction throughout the product's life cycle.

MTBF and MTTR

MTBF (Mean Time Between Failures) and MTTR (Mean Time To Repair) are two important metrics used in reliability engineering and maintenance management.

1. MTBF (Mean Time Between Failures)
 - MTBF refers to the average time interval between consecutive failures of a system or component during normal operation.

- It is calculated by dividing the total operating time by the number of failures that occur within that time period.

- MTBF is a measure of reliability and indicates how long a system or component is expected to operate without experiencing a failure on average.

- A higher MTBF value suggests greater reliability, while a lower MTBF value indicates higher failure rates and reduced reliability.

- MTBF is typically used to assess the reliability of equipment, machinery, or systems and to plan maintenance schedules and spare parts inventory.

2. MTTR (Mean Time To Repair)

- MTTR refers to the average time required to repair a failed system or component and restore it to normal operating condition.

- It is calculated by dividing the total downtime due to repairs by the number of repair incidents.

- MTTR is a measure of maintainability and indicates how quickly a system or component can be restored to service after a failure occurs.

- A lower MTTR value suggests faster repair times and better maintainability, while a higher

MTTR value indicates longer repair times and potentially increased downtime.

- MTTR is used to evaluate maintenance efficiency, identify opportunities for process improvement, and optimize maintenance strategies to minimize downtime and production losses.

Other similar metrics include Mean Time To Failure (MTTF), Mean Time Between Maintenance (MTBM), and Mean Time To Restore Service (MTRS), which are variations or extensions of MTBF and MTTR used in specific contexts or industries.
Reliability of system can be improved by improving reliability of components through better design and sourcing, providing redundancy, preventive maintenance and improving repair capabilities.

Reliability

- < Exercise>
- A product has 3 subcomponents A, B and C. Failure of A can cause the failure of the product. Failure of either only B or C would not cause the failure of the product. However the product fails if both B and C fail simultaneously. The probabilities of A, B and C performing successfully are 0.95, 0.85 and 0.80. What is the reliability of the system?

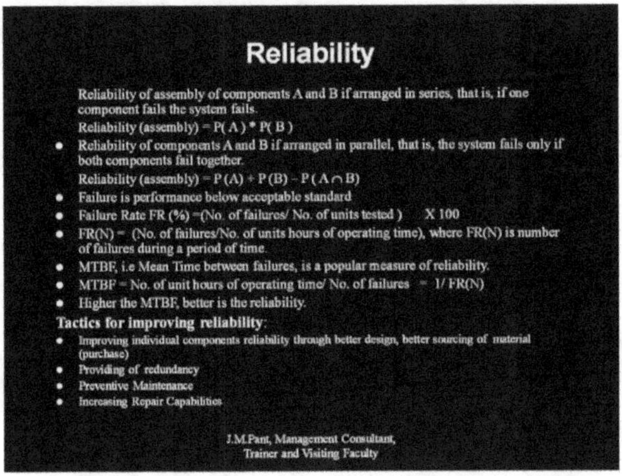

Reliability
Reliability of assembly of components A and B if arranged in series, that is, if one component fails the system fails.
Reliability (assembly) = P(A) * P(B)
Reliability of components A and B if arranged in parallel, that is, the system fails only if both components fail together.
Reliability (assembly) = P (A) + P (B) – P (A ∩ B)
Failure is performance below acceptable standard
Failure Rate FR (%) =(No. of failures/ No. of units tested) X 100
FR(N) = (No. of failures/No. of units hours of operating time), where FR(N) is number of failures during a period of time.
MTBF, i.e Mean Time between failures, is a popular measure of reliability.
MTBF = No. of unit hours of operating time/ No. of failures = 1/ FR(N)
Higher the MTBF, better is the reliability.
Tactics for improving reliability:
Improving individual components reliability through better design, better sourcing of material (purchase)
Providing of redundancy
Preventive Maintenance
Increasing Repair Capabilities
J.M.Pant, Management Consultant,
Trainer and Visiting Faculty

Reliability

- < Exercise>
- Relectro Corporation produces a miniature electric motor consisting of two critical components: coil and prime circuit. Relectro promises its customers a two year motor life with a probability of 0.98. Failure of any of these components renders the motor useless.
- Engineers are considering redesigning and purchasing components from new vendors X and Y. The objective is to meet the customers requirement at minimum cost.
- Data collected is shown in next slide.
- 1. Should the motor be redesigned? Why?
- 2. Recommend the vendor, and compute the reliability and cost of the solution suggested by you.

Reliability

- < Exercise>
- Data collected is as under:
-

Components with existing design	**Unit cost ($)**		**Two year failure probability**	
Coil	17.00		0.01	
Prime Circuit	8.50		0.03	
With new design and new vendors	**Vendor X**	**Vendor Y**	**Vendor X**	**Vendor Y**
Coil	16	21	0.01	0.005
Prime Circuit	12	15	0.02	0.001

I.H.Pant, Management Consultant, Trainer and Visiting Faculty

Maintainability

Maintainability refers to the ease with which the product can be put back into service after a breakdown. Lower the MTTR, better the Maintainability.

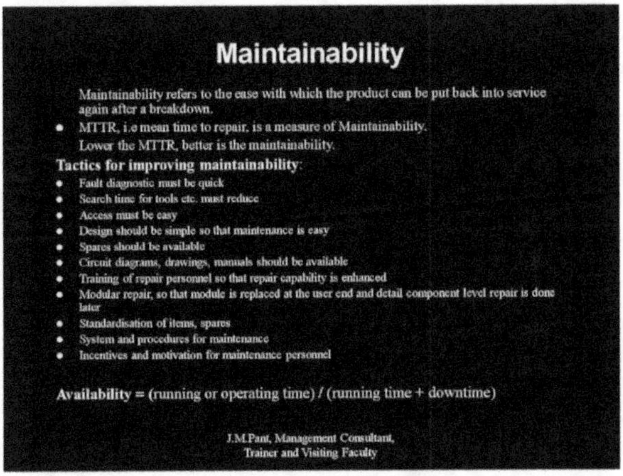

Maintainability
Maintainability refers to the ease with which the product can be put back into service again after a breakdown.
• MTTR, i.e mean time to repair, is a measure of Maintainability.
Lower the MTTR, better is the maintainability.
Tactics for improving maintainability:
• Fault diagnostic must be quick
• Search time for tools etc. must reduce
• Access must be easy
• Design should be simple so that maintenance is easy
• Spares should be available
• Circuit diagrams, drawings, manuals should be available
• Training of repair personnel so that repair capability is enhanced
• Modular repair, so that module is replaced at the user end and detail component level repair is done later
• Standardisation of items, spares
• System and procedures for maintenance
• Incentives and motivation for maintenance personnel
Availability = (running or operating time) / (running time + downtime)
J.M.Pant, Management Consultant,
Trainer and Visiting Faculty

To improve maintainability:

- Fault diagnostics must be quick,
- Availability of manuals, drawings, circuit diagrams.
- Design for maintainability, use and throw, change after specific time.
- Modular design so that modules can be replaced quickly to reduce MTTR, and component level repair done later.

- Easy accessibility of items to be repaired.
- Standardisation of spares, items.
- Availability of spares, tools.
- Reduce search time.
- Trained and experienced engineers and repair crew, incentives and motivation, work culture.

14
Types of Manufacturing Process Flows

Each manufacturing process flow has its advantages and limitations, and the choice of process depends on factors such as product characteristics, production volume, customisation requirements, and industry dynamics. By understanding the different process flows, manufacturers can select the most appropriate approach to meet their specific needs and optimize their operations for efficiency, quality, and competitiveness.

Different ways to organise process flows in manufacturing, and sometimes in services too, are:

1. Project Manufacturing

Project manufacturing is a production method used to create highly customised, one-of-a-kind products or systems that are typically large-scale and complex, like ship building, aircrafts making, infrastructure projects like bridges and flyovers, equipment making like turbines and large boilers, and so forth. Unlike traditional manufacturing processes that focus on mass-producing standardised goods, project manufacturing revolves around the unique requirements of individual projects or contracts having characteristics of customisation, significant variety of size, features, complexity, functionality, uniqueness, long lead times and resource intensive.

2. *Job Shop Manufacturing*

Job shop manufacturing, similar in many points to project but much smaller, involves the production of customised or unique products in small batches or one-off orders.

Each product or order typically requires a unique set of operations, tools, and processes, making job shops highly flexible but often less efficient in terms of production time and cost.

Job shops are commonly found in industries such as fabrication, maintenance and repair shops, and machine shops where each product may have specific requirements or variations.

3. *Batch manufacturing*

Batch manufacturing involves producing a group or batch of identical products in a series of sequential steps.

Products are produced in batches to take advantage of economies of scale while still allowing for some customization or variation within each batch.

Batch manufacturing is suitable for products with moderate demand levels and relatively stable production processes.

Examples include food processing, pharmaceuticals, and electronics assembly.

4. Assembly Line Manufacturing

Assembly line manufacturing involves producing high volumes of standardized products using a linear, sequential production process.

Products move along a conveyor belt or assembly line, with each station performing a specific task or operation.

Assembly line manufacturing is highly efficient and suited for high-volume production of standardized products with minimal variation.

Examples include automobile manufacturing, consumer electronics, and appliances.

5. Flexible Manufacturing Systems (FMS)

Flexible manufacturing systems combine the efficiency of automated production with the flexibility to produce a variety of products in small to medium volumes.

FMS typically consist of computer-controlled machines, robots, and aterial handling systems interconnected by a central control system.

- FMS can quickly switch between different product configurations or designs, making them ideal for industries with rapidly changing demand or short product life cycles.
- Examples include CNC machining centers, 3D printing, and robotic assembly cells.

6. Group Technology Manufacturing

- Group technology manufacturing involves organizing production processes based on the similarities or common characteristics of products.
- Products are grouped into families or clusters based on factors such as size, shape, material, or manufacturing process requirements.
- By grouping similar products together, manufacturers can standardize processes, reduce setup times, and improve efficiency.
- Group technology is commonly used in industries such as metalworking, machining, and assembly operations.

7. Computer Integrated Manufacturing (CIM)

- Computer integrated manufacturing integrates various manufacturing processes, equipment, and systems through computer technology and communication networks.
- CIM systems encompass CAD/CAM software, CNC machines, robotics, PLCs, and other automated systems interconnected with a central control system.
- CIM enables seamless coordination and communication between different stages of the manufacturing process, from design and engineering to production and quality control.
- CIM facilitates real-time monitoring, data analysis, and decision-making, leading to increased productivity, quality, and flexibility.
- CIM is prevalent in industries such as automotive, aerospace, and electronics manufacturing, where high precision, efficiency, and integration are critical.

15
Plant Location

Plant location is a critical decision in operations management, significantly impacting a company's efficiency, costs, and overall success. The process involves selecting a geographical site for establishing a manufacturing facility, considering multiple factors that can affect both operational performance and long-term profitability.

Revenues and cost(fixed and variable) are affected by facility location.
No site will be best in both revenue and cost.
Trade off is necessary.
Plant Location Decision is required when:

- New project
- New product
- Increase in capacity required
- Change in resources (like cost of labour, raw materials, supporting resources (subcontractors) may change)
- Change in demand geographically (for example, North/South, East/West); change in location for better service.

– Change in political and economic conditions.

Preliminary Screening to identify feasible sites

- ***Critical Factors for screening***: These factors are critical, absolutely essential for a site. If not available, then that site should be rejected. For example, electricity for aluminium smelting, fertiliser units; water for photo films, chemical processing unit; ancillary support for automobile unit.
- ***Objective factors***: measurable factors which can be quantified. For example, power tariff, wage rate, cost of land
- ***Subjective factors***: qualitative factors which cannot be measured in numerical terms. For example, industrial relations situation, quality of manpower.

Factoral Analysis:

List all Factors Influencing Plant Location

1.Market nearness-Proximity to Markets and Customer Accessibility.

Being close to key markets reduces transportation costs and delivery times, enhancing customer satisfaction.

-

2.Source proximity and Supply chain Reliability -Availability of Raw Materials, in Quantity and Quality, suppliers and vendors. Locating near raw material sources can lower transportation costs and ensure a steady supply.

Evaluate the reliability and stability of suppliers in the region.

3.Infrastructure and Utilities-Transportation Network: Access to roads, railways, ports, and airports is crucial for efficient and effective logistics. Reliable, adequate and quality supply of electricity, water, and gas is essential for uninterrupted 24/7, 365 day operations. Technology Infrastructure: Availability of communication networks and IT infrastructure.

4.Labour and Professional manpower Availability, quality of manpower and Costs. Skilled Workforce: Access to a pool of skilled and unskilled labour suited to the manufacturing processes, in quality and competency.

Labour Costs: Competitive labour rates balanced with the skill level of the workforce. Labor Laws: Regional labour laws and regulations that could impact operations.

5.Land availability

Clear title, unencumbered, sufficient area, flood history, price.

6.Drainage.

Outside drain should exist and be sufficient in size and capacity to dispose off treated effluents and rain water from plant , so that flooding in plant does not take place.

7.Economic and Political Stability. Government Policies: Incentives, tax breaks, and subsidies offered by local governments. Political Climate: Stability and predictability of the political environment affecting business operations.

8.Environmental Considerations, Compliance and Regulations.
Sustainability: Opportunities for implementing sustainable practices and reducing the environmental footprint.

9.Community, Culture, Housing, Banking, Social Amenities and Quality of Life.
Community Support: Positive relationship with the local community and availability of amenities for employees.
Quality of Life: Access to healthcare, education, schools, housing, and recreational facilities to attract and retain talent.
Positive work culture, productivity of work force.
Bankers, community trade, business, local market associations.

10.Industrial Relations situation, law and order, strikes, go slow.

11.Site feasibility-foe example, no high tension power line overhead, no religious monument, no forest or protected area, no infringement of state/municipal/local authority bye-laws, agricultural land which cannot be converted to industrial use, problems in environment clearance and so forth.

Strategic Implications of Plant Location

1.*Cost Efficiency*

A well-chosen location can significantly reduce operational costs, including transportation, labour, and utilities.

Tax incentives and subsidies can further lower operational expenses.

2.*Operational Efficiency*

Proximity to suppliers and markets enhances the speed and reliability of supply chains.

Better infrastructure supports smoother operations and logistics.

3. *Competitive Advantage*

Strategic location can provide a competitive edge through lower costs and better customer

service.
Access to a skilled workforce and advanced technologies can improve product quality and innovation.

4.*Risk Management*
Diversifying plant locations can mitigate risks associated with regional disruptions, such as natural disasters or political instability.
Assessing environmental impact and adhering to regulations reduces the risk of legal issues.

Tools and Techniques for Plant Location Decision

1.*Factor Rating Method*

Weigh different factors according to their importance and rate each potential location based on these factors to determine the best option.

2.Cost-Profit-Volume Analysis

Analyse the costs associated with each location and the potential revenue to determine the most profitable option.

3. Geographic Information System (GIS)
Use GIS tools to analyse spatial data and visualize the impact of different location factors.

4. Transportation Model
Optimize the transportation costs associated with different locations using linear programming techniques.

5. Break-Even Analysis
Calculate the break-even point for different locations to understand the financial feasibility.

Plant Location: Measures/Models for Evaluation/Analysis

- **Factoral Analysis**

$LM_i = CFM_i * (X * OFM_i + (1 - X) * SFM_i)$

Where LM_i is the location measure index

CFM_i is the critical measure for site i (CFM_i = 0 or 1)

OFM_i is the objective factor measure for site i ($0 \leq OFM_i \leq 1$, $\sum OFM_i = 1$

SFM_i is the subjective factor measure for site i ($0 \leq SFM_i \leq$ =1, $\sum SFM_i$=1

X = objective factor decision weight ($0 \leq X \leq 1$)

(determined by mangement Committee, past data, Delphi method, etc)

Site with largest LM_i is selected

J.M.Pant, Management Consultant, Trainer and Visiting Faculty

Plant Location: Measures/Models for Evaluation/Analysis

- **Break Even Analysis**

(Effect of location on cost and revenues)

Lower the BEP, better is the location

V_{be} (Volume for break even) =

(Fixed cost) / (Sales per unit– Variable cost per unit)

J.M.Pant, Management Consultant, Trainer and Visiting Faculty

Plant Location: Measures/Models for Evaluation/Analysis

- **Simple Median Model**

Minimise Total Transportation Cost = $\sum C_i L_i D_i$

Where L_i is the number of loads to be shipped between facility F_i and the new plant

C_i is the cost to move a load one distance unit from or to F_i

D_i is the distance units between facility F_i and the new plant

$= |x_0 - x_i| + |y_0 - yi|$

assuming loads movement on rectangular paths

J.M.Pant, Management Consultant, Trainer and Visiting Faculty

Plant Location: Measures/Models for Evaluation/Analysis

- **Linear programming – Transportation problem**

A special LP formulation for determining how sources should ship resources to destinations so that the total shipping costs areminimised.

Min TC = $\sum \sum C_{ij}X_{ij}$

X_{ij} = number of resource units allocated from i to j

C_{ij} is the cost of allocating one unit of resource from source i to destination j

J.M.Pant, Management Consultant, Trainer and Visiting Faculty

Plant Location: Exercise

- Factoral Analysis: Exercise - Which is the best site?

Factor	Weight %	Possible Sites(Points Allocated)				
		Noida	Gurgaon	Alwar	Bhopal	Baroda
Market	15	8	8	6	7	7
Sourcing Materials	10	8	8	5	6	8
Manpower Availability	10	9	9	5	6	8
Infrastructure	10	8	8	5	8	8
Labour problems	15	4	6	7	8	9
Cost of land	12	7	6	10	8	6
Cost of utilities	10	5	5	6	6	6
Freight cost	18	6	6	6	6	6

J.M.Pant, Management Consultant,
Trainer and Visiting Faculty

Plant Location: Measures/Models for Evaluation/Analysis

- Break Even Analysis-Exercise-Find the best site

	Site A	Site B	Site C
Selling Price per unit	Rs 50	Rs 50	Rs 50
Fixed cost	Rs 100,000	Rs 120,000	Rs 150,000
Variable cost per unit	Rs 30	Rs 20	Rs 25

J.M.Pant, Management Consultant,
Trainer and Visiting Faculty

Plant Location: Measures/Models for Evaluation/Analysis

- Median Model: Exercise
- Raw material supplies from F1 and F2
- Finished goods to F3 and F4.
- Find location of new plant. Data is as under:

Existing Facility	Loads Li	Cost Ci	Xi, Yi
F1	755	1	20, 30
F2	900	1	10, 40
F3	450	1	30, 50
F4	500	1	40, 60

J.M.Pant, Management Consultant,
Trainer and Visiting Faculty

Plant Location: Measures/Models for Evaluation/Analysis

- Median Model: Exercise
- Find best location for a dairy processing center and compute total cost. Transportation cost Rs 5 per km per 100 kgs..

Location	Milk produced (in 100,000 Kgs)	Xi, Yi (km)
L1	200	20, 0
L2	300	0, 400
L3	800	140, 20
L4	200	360, 80

J.M.Pant, Management Consultant,
Trainer and Visiting Faculty

16
Plant Layout & Material Handling

Plant Layout is the physical location and arrangement of departments, work centers, facilities, equipment, personnel, within a plant or operations facility in their conversion process; spatial arrangement of physical resources including utilities like piping, wiring, cabling, and so forth, to optimize work flow, minimize costs and enhance productivity.

Plant layout is a critical aspect of operations management, influencing the efficiency and effectiveness of manufacturing and service processes.

Layout has to be designed tailor made to operations, broadly categorised as:
Intermittent operations: made to order, batch, low volume, labor intensive products, having more variety in product mix, using general purpose equipments, interrupted product flow and frequent schedule changes
Continuous operations: standardised, high volume, capital intensive products, produce to stock/keep inventory, small variety product

mix, special purpose equipment, and continuous product flow.

Principles and Objectives of Plant Layout

1. ***Optimal Utilisation of Space***: Efficient use of available space to ensure smooth workflow and physical movement. At the same time, adequate open space- for operators, accessibility for maintenance, materials, safe places, storage, work in progress, aisles, and to avoid congestion

2. ***Minimisation of Material Handling and Personnel Movement Costs***: Reducing the distance and time required to move materials between different stages of production. Moving shortest possible distance and avoiding backtracking and criss cross flows.

3. ***Enhanced Workflow and Efficiency***: Streamlining processes to avoid bottlenecks and delays. Smooth production flow following the Standard Operations Process. Should be easy to manage and supervise and oversee operations.

4. ***Improved Employee Morale and Safety***: Creating a safe and comfortable working

environment. All safety and fire prevention and extinguishing provisions as per law and otherwise should be provided for.

5. ***Flexibility and Scalability***: Designing layouts that can adapt to changes in production processes or product lines. Flexibility and provision for expansion and scaling up capacity.

6.***Environment impact*** taken care of. This includes providing space for facilities for pollution control-air, effluents, solids; health and hygiene, illumination and ventilation.

7.***Fulfillment of Statutory and legal*** requirements including offsets and distance from gas facilities, creche and canteen , toilets and so forth.

Types of Plant Layout (see Appendix for diagrams)

Process Oriented or Functional Layout: Grouping similar processes or machines and equipment together according to their function.

Suitable for job shops or batch production where customization is high, and production volumes are low.

Flexibility in production, specialisation of labour, and ease of supervision, are the merits. The disadvantages are high material handling costs, complex scheduling, and longer production times.

Product oriented or Line Layout

Arranging equipment and workstations in an order that matches the sequence of tasks of the production process. The arrangement could be linear, circular, U shape or another depending on the nature of process and space available.
Line layout is deal for mass production or assembly lines where products are standardised. The advantages are lower material handling costs, reduced production time, and high output.
The demerits are inflexibility to changes, high initial setup costs, and dependency on balanced production lines.

Fixed layout

The arrangement of facilities so that product is stationary, that is, stays in one location; and workers, materials, tools, equipment, are brought to it as needed (for example, ships, aircrafts)

The fixed layout is used for large, bulky products such as ships, aircraft, turbines or project type large equipment building and construction.
The layout provides flexibility to project specifications, and reduced movement of the product. The disadvantages are high transportation costs for materials and equipment, and complex scheduling

Combination layout

A hybrid approach that combines elements of process, product, and fixed-position layouts. Suitable for facilities producing a variety of products or using different production methods. The advantages are greater flexibility and efficiency, and the ability to handle a diverse range of products. But the demerit is the complexity in design and management, and potential for higher costs.

Cellular layout

Grouping different machines into cells, each of which can handle a specific set of operations. Arrangement of facilities so that equipment used to make similar parts or families of parts are grouped together.

This is suitable for batch production with similar processes. The advantage is reduced material handling, increased flexibility, and better utilisation of equipment and labour. The disadvantage is that the initial setup and training can be costly, and balancing workload among cells can be challenging.

Factors Influencing Plant Layout

1.***Nature of Product***: The size, shape, and type of product significantly influence the layout design.

2.***Production Volume and nature of Operations.***: High-volume production favours product layouts, while low-volume, customised production suits process layouts. The specific processes and equipment required impact the layout choice.

3.***Space Availability***: The physical space constraints and expansion potential of the facility.

4.***Material Handling***: Efficient movement and storage of materials to minimize costs and delays.

5.***Optimal workforce and Equipment***

Utilisation:; complying with safety, health, environment standards and statutory laws.

6..***Future Expansion***: The ability to adapt the layout for future growth or changes in production.

Steps in Designing a Plant Layout

1.***Define Objectives***: Clearly outline the goals and requirements of the layout.

2.***Analyse Production and Operations*** Process: Understand the workflow, processes, SOPs, sequence and interdependencies.

3.***Gather Data***: Collect information on space requirements, equipment specifications, material flow, and labour needs.

4.***Create multiple layout options*** based on different scenarios and constraints.

5.***Evaluate Alternatives***: Assess each layout option against the objectives and criteria such as cost, efficiency, and flexibility.

6. ***Select the Best Layout***: Choose the layout that best meets the objectives and constraints.

7.***Implement the Layout***: Plan and execute the layout, including moving equipment and setting up workstations, provision for utilities.

8.***Review and Improve***: Continuously

monitor the layout's performance and make necessary Improvements and Adjustments.

Tools and Techniques for Plant Layout

1.***Flowcharts and Diagrams***: Visual representations of the production process and material flow through Process Flow Charts, Travel chart, and String diagram.
2.***Computer-Aided Design (CAD)***: Software tools for creating detailed layout designs.
3.***Simulation Software***: Tools to model and test different layout scenarios and their impact on plant performance and productivity.
4. ***Material Handling Analysis***: Assessing the movement and storage of materials to optimise efficiency through simplification, elimination or changing from serial to parallel sequence..
5.***Queuing Theory***: Analysing and managing waiting lines and workflow to reduce bottlenecks.

Plant layout is a vital component of operations management, directly affecting the efficiency, cost-effectiveness, and scalability of manufacturing processes. By carefully considering factors such as product nature, production volume, and space availability, and employing tools and techniques like CAD and simulation software, organisations can design effective layouts that enhance productivity and support business growth. Continuous review and improvement of the plant layout ensure that it remains aligned with evolving operational needs and market demands.

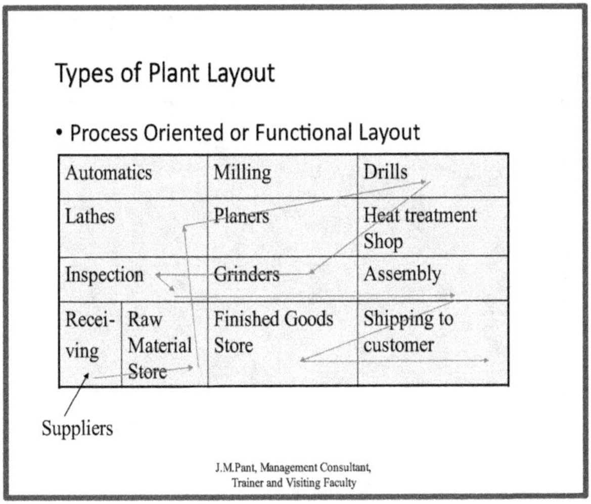
Types of Plant Layout
• Process Oriented or Functional Layout
Automatics
Milling
Drills
Lathes
Planers
Heat treatment Shop
Inspection
Grinders
Assembly
Recei-ving
Raw Material Store
Finished Goods Store
Shipping to customer
Suppliers
J.M.Pant, Management Consultant, Trainer and Visiting Faculty

Types of Plant Layout

- Product or Line Layout

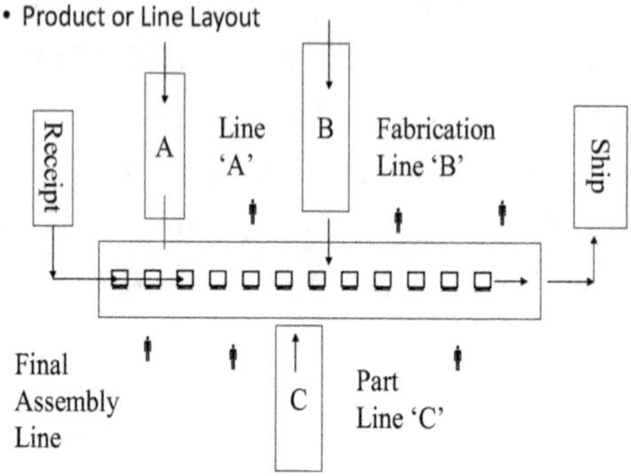
Receipt
A
Line
'A'
B
Fabrication
Line 'B'
Ship
Final
Assembly
Line
C
Part
Line 'C'

J.M.Pant, Management Consultant,
Trainer and Visiting Faculty

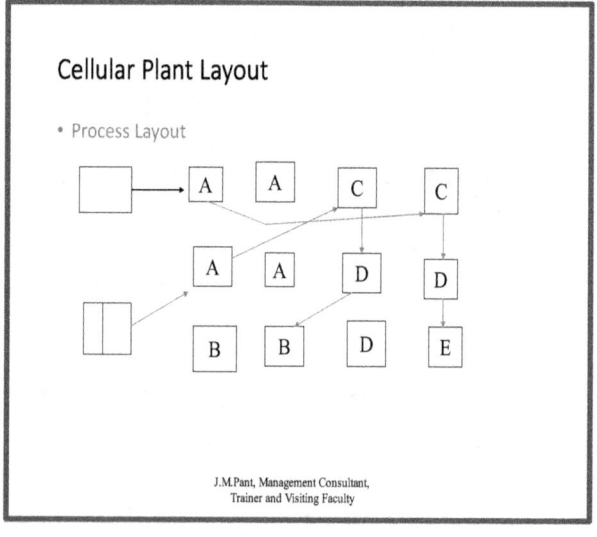

Cellular Plant Layout

- Process Layout

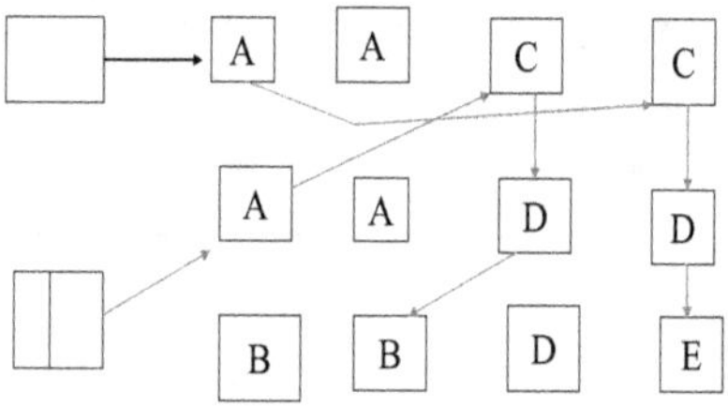
A
A
C
C
A
A
D
D
B
B
D
E

J.M.Pant, Management Consultant,
Trainer and Visiting Faculty

Cellular Plant Layout

- Cellular Layout

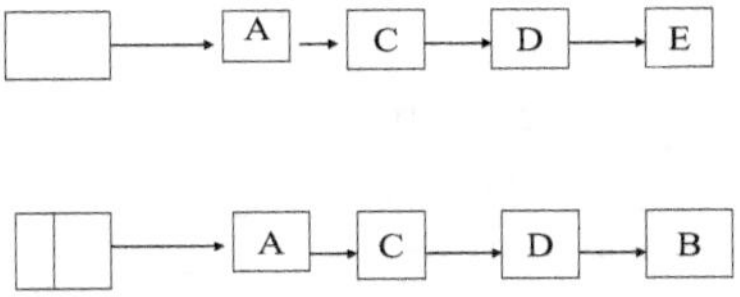
A
C
D
E
A
C
D
B

J.M.Pant, Management Consultant,
Trainer and Visiting Faculty

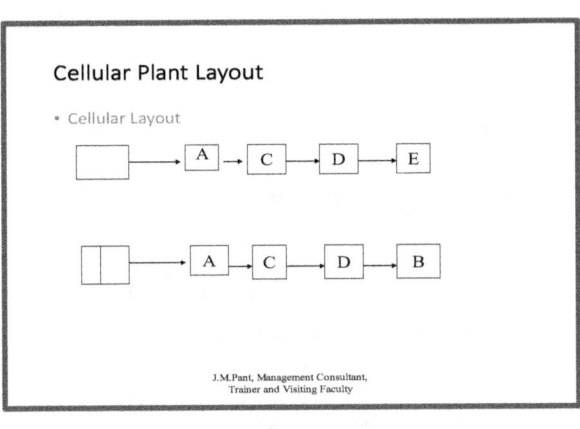

Comparison of Different Types of Plant Layout

Layout

	Product	Process	Fixed
Product	Standard,large volume,stable rate of output	Diversified product, varying volume	Made to order, low volume
Work Flow	Sequential/linear, for each unit the same sequence	Variable flow. Different sequence	No flow. Equipment, men, brought to site
Human Skills	Routine/repetitive	Adaptable high skills	High skills, flexibility
Production Planning and Control	Easy	Complex	Complex
Material Handling	Automated	Duplicate handling	General equipment, heavy duty
Inventory	Medium raw material and WIP	High raw material and WIP	High inventories
Space Utilization	Efficient	Medium	Medium
Capital Requirement	Large specialised equipment	General purpose	General purpose, mobile
Product Cost	High fixed cost but low unit cost	Low fixed cost but high unit cost	Low fixed cost but high unit cost
Behavioral	Job dissatisfaction, routine, absenteeism, employee turnover	Managers skilled in inter group coordination	Managers skilled in project management

J.M.Pant, Management Consultant,
Trainer and Visiting Faculty

- Load Distance Model

$$\text{Minimise cost } C = \left(\sum_{i=1}^{n}\sum_{j=1}^{n} L_{ij} D_{ij}\right)k$$

n=number of work centers

L_{ij} = number of loads between work centers i and j

D_{ij} = distance between work center i and j

K= cost to move load one distance unit

Computer Model –CRAFT: Computerised Relative Allocation of Facilities Techniques

J.M.Pant, Management Consultant,
Trainer and Visiting Faculty

Travel Chart

- For material movement analysis, for relationship among activities. This helps in plant layout.
- Example:

	Casting	Drilling	Machining	Welding	Inspection	Total
Casting		5	8	2	8	23
Drilling			2		8	10
Machining		3		2	5	10
Welding					6	6
Inspection						
Total		8	10	4	27	49 / 49

J.M.Pant, Management Consultant,
Trainer and Visiting Faculty

Templates for Layout

Use of templates, String Diagram

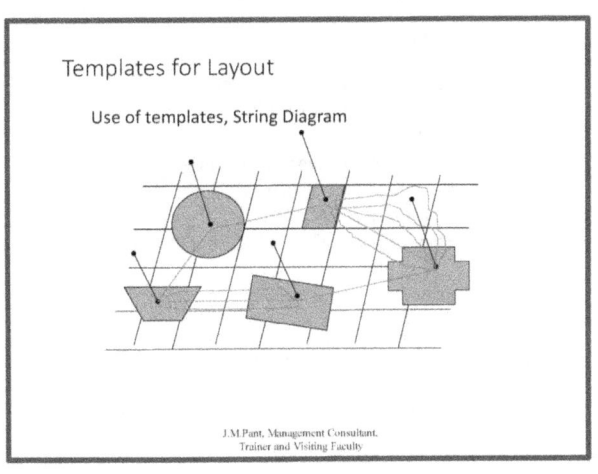

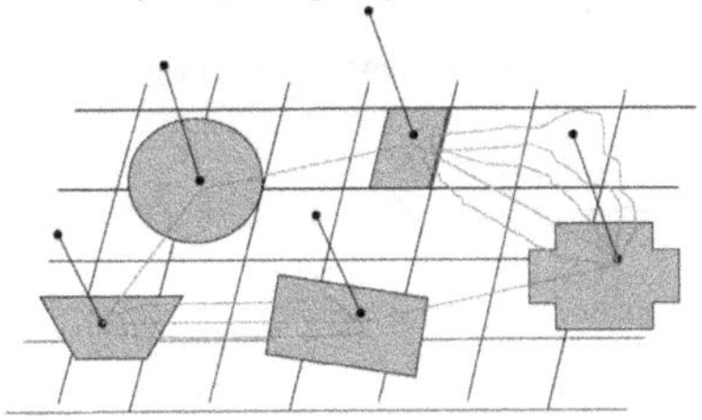

J.M.Pant, Management Consultant,
Trainer and Visiting Faculty

Templates for Layout

- Three Dimensional blocks

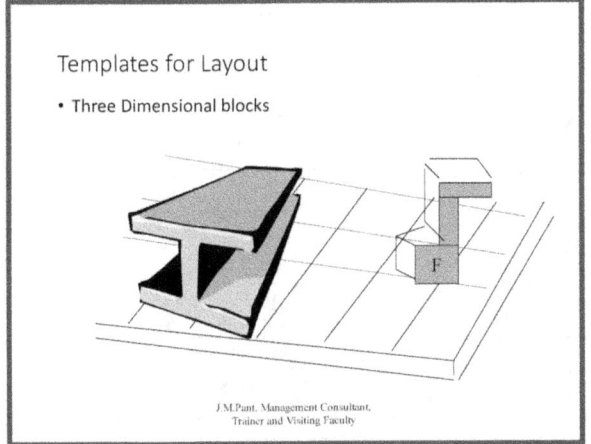

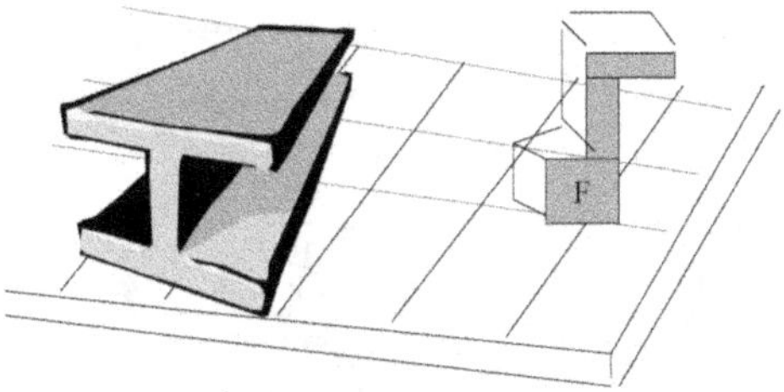
F

J.M.Pant, Management Consultant,
Trainer and Visiting Faculty

Modelling Product Layout

- Heuristic:A procedure in which a set of rules is systematically applied-an algorithm
- ① Is capacity adequate?
- Bottleneck operation- longest task time.
- Cycle time- time elapsing between completed units coming off an assembly line
- Maximum daily output = Available Time/Cycle time per unit
- <Example> Flow line for making aluminum windows

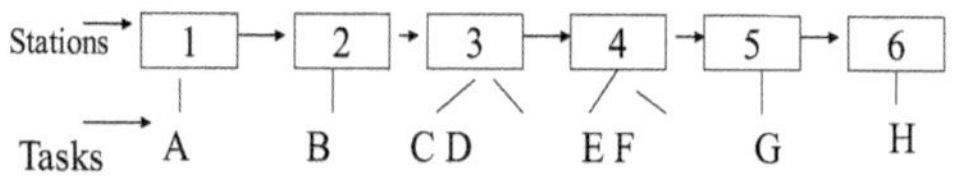
Stations
1
2
3
4
5
6
Tasks
A
B
C D
E F
G
H

J.M.Pant, Management Consultant,
Trainer and Visiting Faculty

Modelling Product Layout

- Desired Minimum Daily Output Capacity-320 windows (8 hours working per day)

Work Station	Preceding Work Station	Tasks Assigned	Prede-cessor	Task Time (secs)
1	-	A: Assemble frame	None	70
2	1	B:Instal Rubber Moulding	A	80
3	2	C:Insert frame screws	A	40
		D;Instal frame latch	A	20
4	3	E:Instal frame handle	A	40
		F:Instal Glass Pane	B,C	30
5	4	G:Cover frame screws	C	50
6	5	H: Pack window frame unit	D,E,F,G	50

J.M.Pant, Management Consultant,
Trainer and Visiting Faculty

Modelling Product Layout

- Longest time is at Station 2- 80 secs – ***bottleneck operation***
- ***Cycle time is 80 secs***
- Output = 8hrsX 60X 60/80 = 360 units
- Required is 320 units daily. So capacity is adequate.
- ② Is sequence of tasks feasible?
- Yes, it is, as the precedence requirements are maintained.

J.M.Pant, Management Consultant,
Trainer and Visiting Faculty

Modelling Product Layout

- ③ Is the line efficient?
- Calculate idleness of man and machine. Idle time will increase cost which ultimately may make the unit non competitive.
- **Balancing the Line**
- Line balancing problem is assigning tasks among workers in the assembly line stations so that performance times are made as equal as possible.
- **Longest Operation Time (LOT) Rule: A line balancing heuristic that gives top assignment priority to the task that has longest operation time.**

J.M.Pant, Management Consultant,
Trainer and Visiting Faculty

Modelling Product Layout

- **Balancing the Line: Six Steps**
- 1. Define tasks
- 2. Identify precedence relationships
- 3. Calculate minimum number of stations required to produce desired output
- 4. Apply the LOT rule to assign tasks to each station
- 5. Evaluate effectiveness and efficiency
- 6. Seek further improvement

J.M.Pant, Management Consultant,
Trainer and Visiting Faculty

Modelling Product Layout

- **Balancing the Line: Window frame assembly example**
- Find minimum number of stations:
- Min. no.stations = Total processing time/Cycle time
- Time required = sum of total time of tasks= Sum of time for A to H tasks= 380 seconds
- If cycle time is 90 secs, minimum no. of stations= 380/90= 4.22 I.e 5 stations.
- If cycle time is 80 secs, no. of stations = 380/80 =5
- Actual layout may need more because of precedence requirements.
- Initial layout uses 6 work stations.

J.M.Pant, Management Consultant,
Trainer and Visiting Faculty

Modelling Product Layout

- Balancing the Line: Window frame assembly example
- LOT 1: assign first the task that takes the most time to the first station. Maintain precedence requirements.
- LOT 2: After assigning a task, determine how much time the station has left to contribute (Time minus Task Times)
- LOT 3: If the station can contribute more time, assign it a task requiring as much time as possible. Maintain precedence relationship. Else return to LOT 1 and continue until all the tasks have been assigned to stations.

J.M.Pant, Management Consultant,
Trainer and Visiting Faculty

Modelling Product Layout

- Balancing the Line: Window frame assembly example
- Solution for 90 sec cycle time:
- 5 work stations: AD B CG EF H
- Efficiency=(380/450) * 100 = 84.4%
- Initial 6 work stations, efficiency was (380/540)*100= 70.4 %.
- Find the solution for 80 second cycle time.

J.M.Pant, Management Consultant,
Trainer and Visiting Faculty

Material Handling

Material handling is the function of moving the right material to the right place in the right time, in the right amount, in sequence, and in the right condition to minimize production and service cost.

Objectives of Material Handling:

1. To increase efficiency of material flow by ensuring availability of materials when & where they needed
2. To reduce Material Handling cost
3. To improve facilities utilization
4. To improve safety & working conditions
5. To facilitate manufacturing processes
6. To increase productivity.

Unit Load Concept

Unit Load is number of items arranged such that they can be handled as a single object. Unit load can be accomplished by:

1. Palletization: It is assembling & securing of individual items on a platform that can be moved by a truck or a crane.
2. Unitisation: It is also the assembling of goods, but as one compact load. Unlike

palletisation additional materials are used for packaging & wrapping the items as a complete unit.

3. Containerisation: It is assembling of items in a box or a bin. It is most suitable for use with conveyors, trailers, transportation by ships.

Pallet

Principles of Material Handling

(1).Planning: maximum overall equipment effectiveness.

1.Equipment selection, Capacity, Standardisation, Flexibility, Dead weight(Reduce the ratio of dead weight of mobile handling equipment to load carried), Reliability, Performance, Safety, Maintainability.

2.Utilisation of equipments; Availability; remove obsolete ones.

3.Maintenance: routine, preventive, predictive

(2)System Flow: Integrate handling covering vendor, receiving, storage, production, inspection, packaging, warehousing, shipping, transportation, & customer.

(3)Material Flow: Provide an operation sequence & equipment layout optimising material flow.

(4)Simplification: Reduce, eliminate, combine movements.

(5)Gravity: Use gravity, reducing energy and equipment.

(6)Space utilisation : Volumetric efficiency, use vertical space, compact equipment, can move in narrow spaces, cover heights.

(7)Unit size: increase size, weight, quantity, flow rate
(8)Mechanise
(9)Automation.

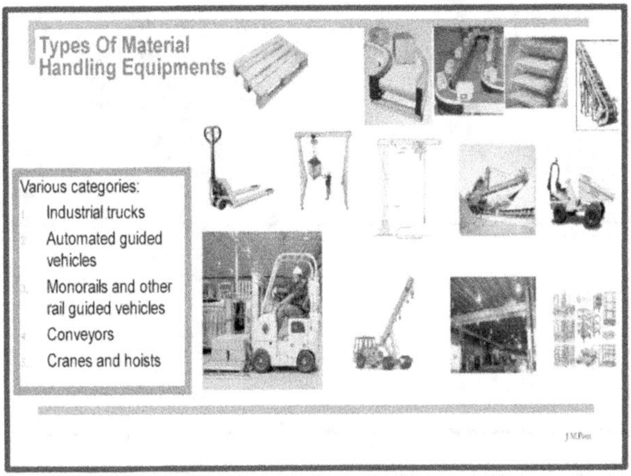

Types Of Material Handling Equipments
Various categories:
1. Industrial trucks
2. Automated guided vehicles
3. Monorails and other rail guided vehicles
4. Conveyors
5. Cranes and hoists

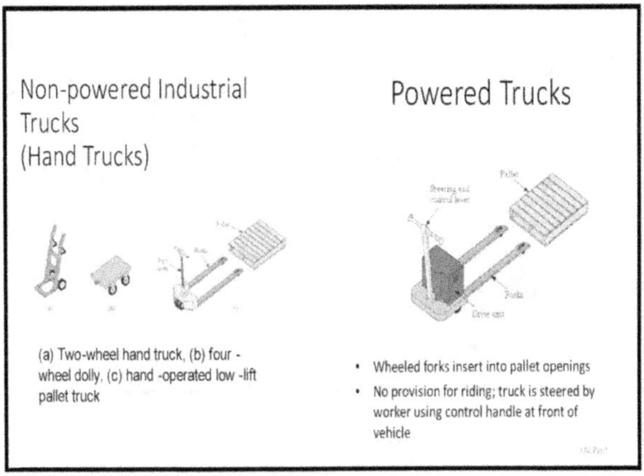

Non-powered Industrial Trucks (Hand Trucks)
(a) Two-wheel hand truck, (b) four -wheel dolly, (c) hand -operated low -lift pallet truck
Powered Trucks
Pallet
Forks
Drive unit
Wheeled forks insert into pallet openings
No provision for riding; truck is steered by worker using control handle at front of vehicle

ForkLifts- Powered Trucks

- Widely used in factories and warehouses because pallet loads are so common
- Power sources include on-board batteries and diesel engines.

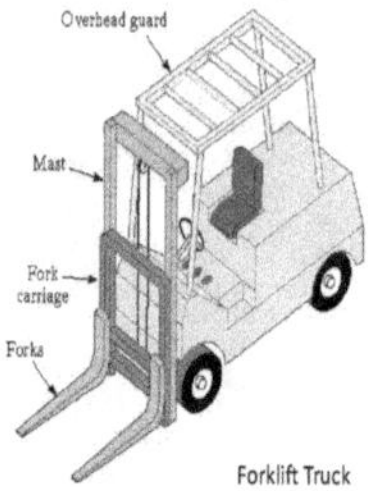
Overhead guard
Mast
Fork carriage
Forks

Forklift Truck

Powered Trucks

- Designed to pull one or more trailing carts in factories and warehouses, as well as for airport baggage handling
- Powered by on-board batteries or IC engines

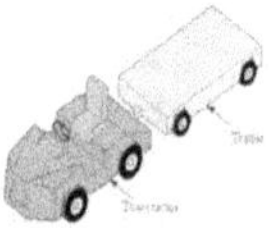

Towing Tractor

Trailer Trains

Driverless Automated Guided Train

- Common application is moving heavy payloads over long distances in warehouses and factories without intermediate stops along the route

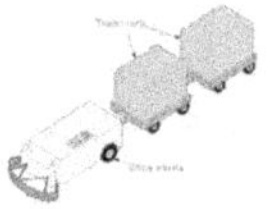

Automated Guided Vehicle System (AGVS) Pallet Truck

Used to move palletized loads along predetermined routes.

Vehicle is backed into loaded pallet by worker; pallet is then elevated from floor.

Worker drives pallet truck to AGV guide path and programs destination.

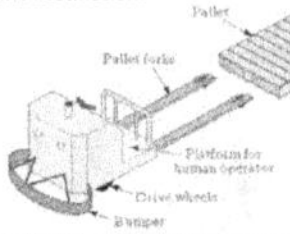

Overhead Trolley Conveyor

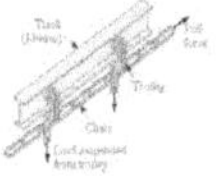

Overhead Monorail

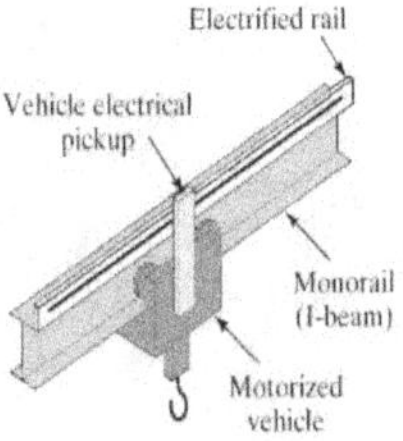
Electrified rail
Vehicle electrical pickup
Monorail (I-beam)
Motorized vehicle

Jib Crane

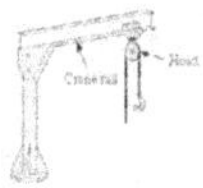

Bridge Crane

Gantry Crane

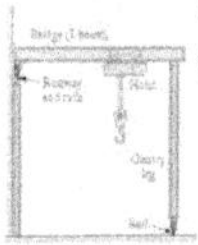

Roller Conveyor

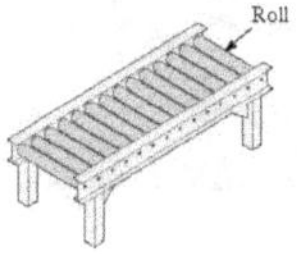
Roll

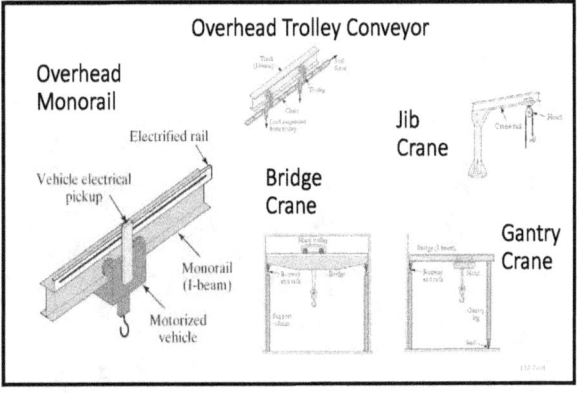

- Powered rollers rotate to drive the loads forward
- Un-powered roller conveyors also available

Belt Conveyor

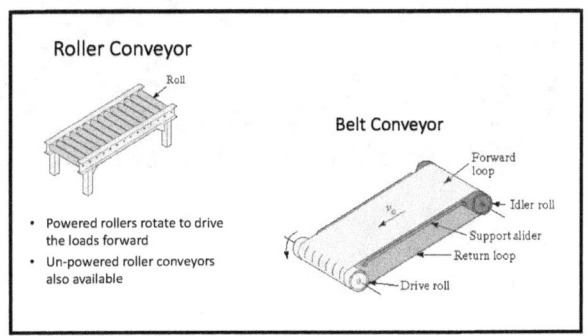

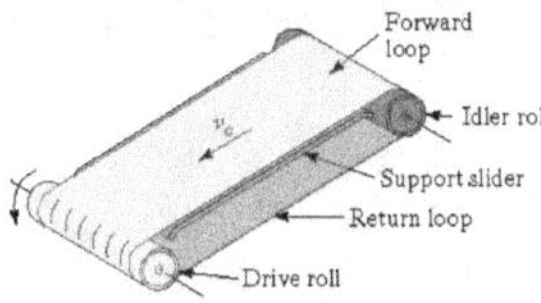
Forward loop
Idler roll
Support slider
Return loop
Drive roll

17
Capacity-Plant, Services

Capacity refers to the maximum output that a plant or an organisation can produce in a given period with the available resources.

Effective capacity planning ensures that a company can meet current and future demands efficiently and economically

Capacity: Maximum productive capability in volume of output per unit time.

Need for capacity planning

When you decide to produce more to meet customer demand.

When you decide to add a new product.

When you change your product mix.

Measures of Capacity

In units of tons, numbers (of cars).

In megawatts (for power plant).

In number of seats (airlines, educational institutions, restaurant).

In number of beds (hospitals, hotels).

In cubic feet of storage space (warehouse).

Capacity affects:

Cost efficiency of operations.

Scheduling of output.

Cost of maintaining facility.

Capacity build up requires investment

Conduct investment analysis.

ROI, IRR, Payback, Break Even point.

Too much capacity requires ways to reduce capacity- such as temporarily closing, selling.

Capacity and Location

Centralised in one place.

Spread over different locations.

Types of Capacity

Design Capacity: The theoretical maximum output under ideal conditions.

Effective Capacity: The maximum output that can be realistically achieved, considering constraints such as maintenance, downtime, and quality standards.

Actual Capacity: The actual output achieved, which can be lower than effective capacity due to unexpected issues.

Capacity Planning

***Short-term Planning*:** Addresses immediate needs, often focusing on scheduling, labour allocation, and resource utilization.

Medium-term Planning: Involves adjustments over several months, including workforce changes and minor equipment purchases.
Long-term Planning: Strategic decisions over years, involving major investments in facilities, equipment, and technology.

Capacity Utilisation

The ratio of actual output to design capacity, indicating how well resources are used.
Utilization=
((Actual Output)/(Design Capacity)) * 100

Efficiency: The ratio of actual output to effective capacity, reflecting operational performance.
Efficiency=
((Actual Output)/(Effective Capacity)) * 100

Factors Affecting Capacity

Demand Fluctuations: Seasonal variations, market trends, and customer preferences.
Technological Changes: Advancements can increase capacity but require investment.

Labour Force: Availability, skill levels, and productivity of the workforce.
Supply Chain: Reliability of suppliers and logistics capabilities.
Maintenance: Regular upkeep to prevent downtime and maintain quality.

Capacity Strategies

Lead Strategy: Adding capacity in anticipation of demand growth.

Lag Strategy: Adding capacity only after demand has exceeded current capacity.

Match Strategy: Incrementally adding capacity to match demand increases.

Adjustment Strategy: Flexible and responsive changes to capacity based on short-term demand shifts; flexible work force levels through hiring and layoff; maintaining a backlog of orders; subcontracting; .

Inventory build up: Produce to capacity and retain excess production over demand during lean period as inventory, and this inventory can be used to meet demand during peak demand periods.

Improvement in Productivity to generate more useful capacity: Process design, Kaizen, Increase Utilisation of equipment and workforce; workforce training; better maintenance management through TPM,

Capacity in Manufacturing

Production Line Balancing: Ensuring that each stage of production is synchronized to prevent bottlenecks.

Inventory Management: Balancing between holding costs and stockouts to optimize production.

Lean Manufacturing: Reducing waste and improving process efficiencies to enhance capacity utilization.

Capacity in Services

Service Design: Structuring services to manage customer flow and service time.

Workforce Management: Scheduling and training employees to meet service demands efficiently.

Technology Integration: Using software and automation to improve service delivery and capacity.

Tools and Techniques for Capacity Planning

Forecasting: Predicting future demand to plan capacity needs.

Queuing Theory: Analysing wait times and service efficiency in service operations.

Simulation Models: Creating models to test different capacity scenarios and outcomes.

Break-Even Analysis: Determining the level of production needed to cover costs and achieve profitability.

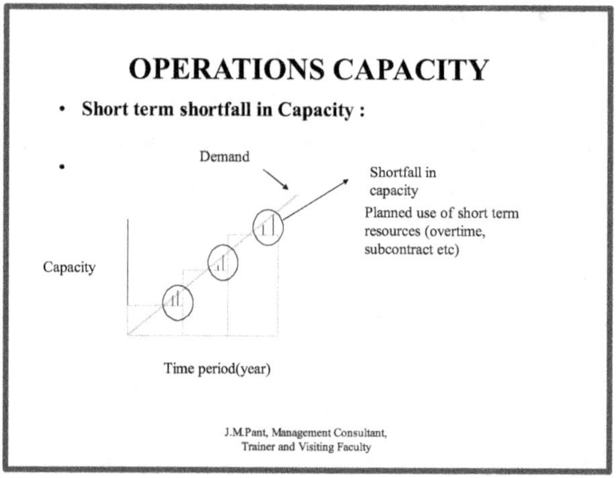

OPERATIONS CAPACITY
Short term shortfall in Capacity :
Demand
Shortfall in capacity
Planned use of short term resources (overtime, subcontract etc)
Capacity
Time period(year)
J.M.Pant, Management Consultant, Trainer and Visiting Faculty

OPERATIONS CAPACITY

- Production cost related to factory's facility capacity.

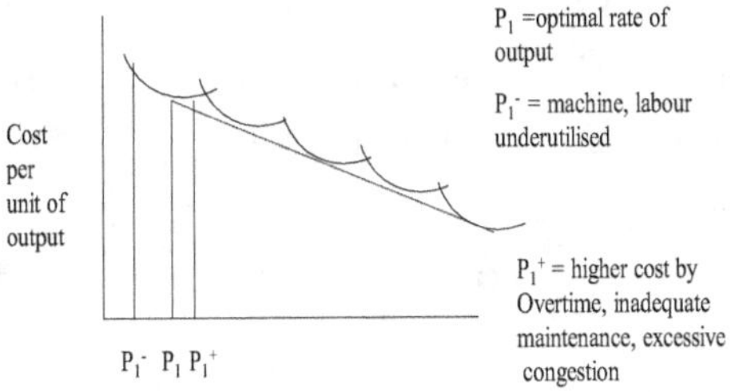

P_1 =optimal rate of output
P_1^- = machine, labour underutilised
Cost per unit of output
P_1^+ = higher cost by Overtime, inadequate maintenance, excessive congestion
P_1^- P_1 P_1^+

J.M.Pant, Management Consultant, Trainer and Visiting Faculty

OPERATIONS CAPACITY

- **Capacity build up options:**
- Step wise increase
- Increase in one go

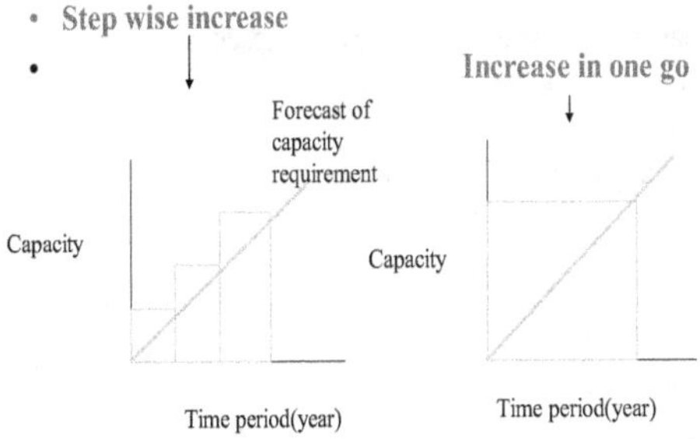

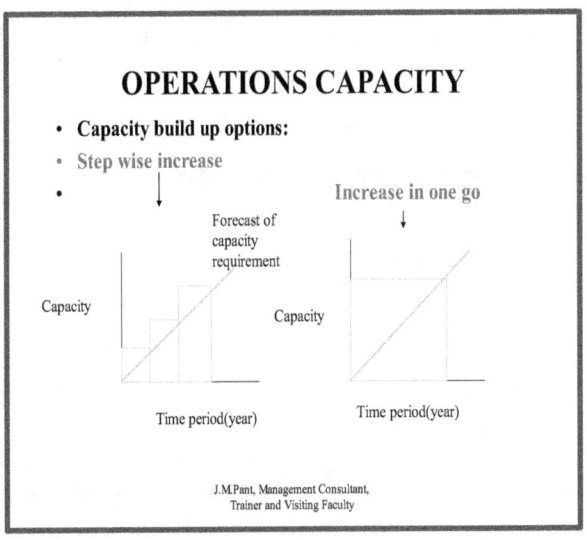

Forecast of capacity requirement
Capacity
Time period(year)
Capacity
Time period(year)

J.M.Pant, Management Consultant, Trainer and Visiting Faculty

Steps to Capacity Planning

① Assessing existing capacity, ②Forecasting capacity needs:. Using forecasting methods, market analysis, product life cycle, technology etc.③Identifying alternate ways to modify capacity, ④ Evaluating alternatives (financial, economical, technological), ⑤ Selecting capacity alternative most suited to achieve strategic mission, ⑥Decide on plan for implementation.

OPERATIONS CAPACITY

- **Short term strategies for modifying capacity**

1. Inventories

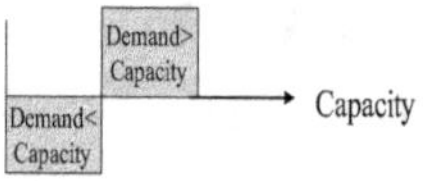
Demand> Capacity
Demand< Capacity
Capacity

2. Backlog –order booking excess of capacity and keep an order backlog file. For example, Maruti cars; service units
3. Employment levels - hire, layoff
4. Work force utilization
5. Employee training
6. Process design
7. Subcontracting
8. Maintenance

J.M.Pant, Management Consultant, Trainer and Visiting Faculty

OPERATIONS CAPACITY

- **Decision Tree Analysis**
- **Decision Tree**
- A diagram used to structure and analyze a decision problem; a systematic, sequential laying out of decision points, alternatives and chance events.
- **Chance event**
- An event leading potentially to several different outcomes, only one of which will definitely occur ; the decision maker has no control over which outcome will occur.

□ Decision point
○ Chance Event
Alternatives

J.M.Pant, Management Consultant,
Trainer and Visiting Faculty

OPERATIONS CAPACITY

- **Decision Tree Analysis**
- **Decision Tree**

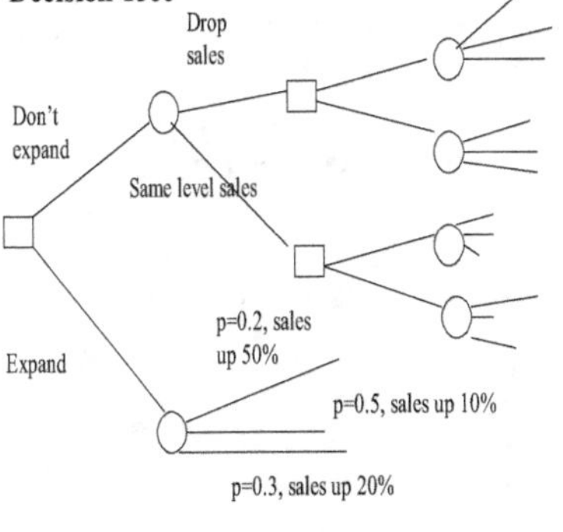
Drop
sales
Don't
expand
Same level sales
Expand
p=0.2, sales
up 50%
p=0.5, sales up 10%
p=0.3, sales up 20%

J.M.Pant, Management Consultant,
Trainer and Visiting Faculty

Make or Buy Decision: Factors to consider.

Quality considerations. If inhouse capability is not enough to produce the desired quality, then buy and outsource. If quality of subcontractor or vendor is not adequate, it is better to Make.

Quantity considerations. Check the criteria of Volume, Scale and Scalability-to decide on inhouse manufacturing or outsourcing.

Cost considerations. Check whether cost is lower making in plant or buying it from others.

Service considerations. Check whether assured supply of items to production line, and speed of delivery is better achieved through making in plant or buying it from outside.

Availability of technical knowhow, technical and management skills- Check whether it is available within or outside.

Save investment cost. If you buy from outside, you will save capital expenditure in creating assets to make that item.

Manage Short term overloads in capacity. Buying from others can help in managing the demand overload without creating capacity which will appear wasted once the demand declines.

Capacity has to be a long term decision though it may be built in phases. As capacity of most plants and services has a human element, it becomes difficult to estimate it. Capacity estimates are based on many assumptions which can be challenged. That is why one reads in some annual reports a 110% capacity utilisation though mathematically it can't exceed 100%. The constraints can be overcome. As capacity is decided by the weakest link, effort should be made on complementing that.

Theory of Constraints and the Goal

Eliyahu Goldratt, formulated postulates on capacity, constraints and scheduling penned down in a story telling and Socrates style questioning format in his famous book 'The Goal' and 'Theory Of Constraints (TOC).'

The Goal, according to Goldratt, is to make a profit. The financial performance measures of importance are net profit, ROI and cash flow. For the operations person, the operation measurements are:

①Throughput (T), ②Inventory (I) and ③Operational Expense (OE).

Throughput is defined as the rate at which the system generates money through sales (not production). Inventory is all the money that the system invests in purchasing things which it intends to sell. This does not include labour and overhead. Operational Expense is all the money the system spends in order to turn inventory into throughput. This includes all the other expenses, including direct labour.

Net profit = Throughput – Operating Expense , that is, T – OE

ROI = (T-OE)/I

These measures are defined this way to focus decision making on activities that will improve the goal of making a profit. Because it has the greatest impact on net profit and ROI, throughput is elevated to the most important measure.

The Capacity thereby gets defined by the Throughput and is limited by the constraints. The critical path defines the capacity. It happens to be the capacity of the weakest link in the chain. Identify that through the five focusing steps and continuously eliminate or reduce the constraints to enhance the capacity.

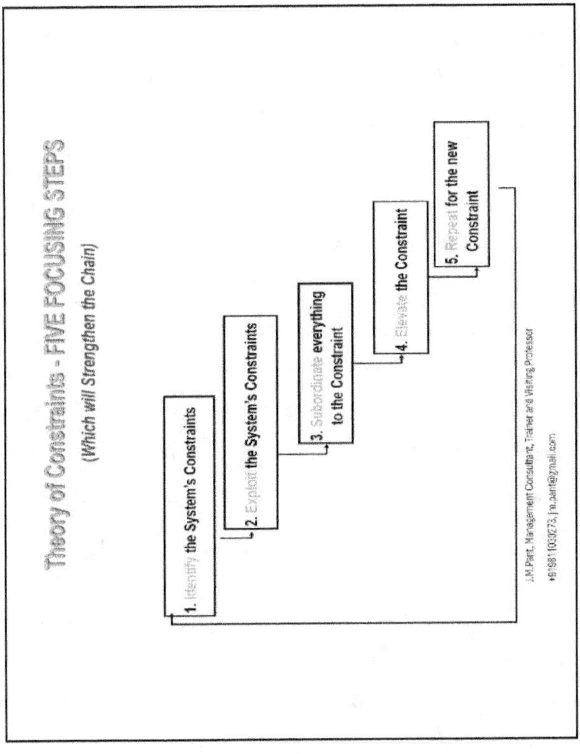
Theory of Constraints - FIVE FOCUSING STEPS
(Which will Strengthen the Chain)
1. Identify the System's Constraints
2. Exploit the System's Constraints
3. Subordinate everything to the Constraint
4. Elevate the Constraint
5. Repeat for the new Constraint
J.M.Pant, Management Consultant, Trainer and Visiting Professor
+919811030273, jm.pant@gmail.com

Bottlenecks

Any resource whose capacity is equal to or less than the demand placed upon it.

Non-bottlenecks

A resource whose capacity is greater than the demand placed upon it.

One should utilise the full existing capacity of the bottleneck resources at all times. Bottlenecks should not sit idle at any time, lunch breaks should be adjusted so that the machines keep running during that time.

An hour lost at a bottleneck is an hour lost in the whole system's capacity.

Increasing the capacity of the bottleneck resources requires offloading the bottleneck by dividing the work between more machines, providing them with work only which must pass through it (that has been cleared by quality), prioritizing as per due dates and tagging parts accordingly, and working only on what contributes to the throughput *that day.*

In short, the bottleneck machine must keep running and Kaizen and other improvements must be done on the bottleneck.

18
Production Planning, Scheduling and Control

Production Planning and Control (PPC) concerns with volume and timing of outputs; matching of resources namely materials, manpower and equipment to meet desired output as per schedule; utilization of operations capacity to the maximum and balancing outputs with capacity; maintaining cost effectiveness and meeting customer's schedule deadlines.

PPC is planning production, fixing route/sequence, scheduling (start and end timings) and follow up.

Planning function includes planning, loading, routing, scheduling, process planning, material planning, tool planning, demand forecasting, and inventory planning

Control function includes coordinating entire production, sales, stores, link to all functions, progressing, follow up, expediting, material control, inventory control, ensuring production targets, delivery deadlines, and capacity utilization

Production planning, scheduling, and control are integral components of operations management, ensuring that manufacturing processes are efficient, cost-effective, and capable of meeting customer demands. Material Requirements Planning (MRP) is a crucial aspect of this, providing a framework for managing inventory, production schedules, and procurement activities.

A good planning system must answer:
What are we going to make?- customer demand.
What does it take to make?-process plan.
What do we have?-capacity, resources.
What do we need?-to fulfill customer requirements.
Questions of priority (what products, how many, when, they are needed) and capacity, and need to balance the two

Objectives of Production Planning and Control

1.Meeting Customer Demand: Ensuring that

products are available to meet customer requirements.
2.Optimizing Resource Utilization: Efficient use of materials, labour, and machinery.
3.Minimising Costs: Reducing inventory, production, and operational costs.
4. Ensuring Quality: Maintaining the desired quality standards in production.
5. Adapting to Changes: Flexibility to adjust to changes in demand, supply, and production capacity., and developing a plan to produce goods in the most efficient and effective manner.

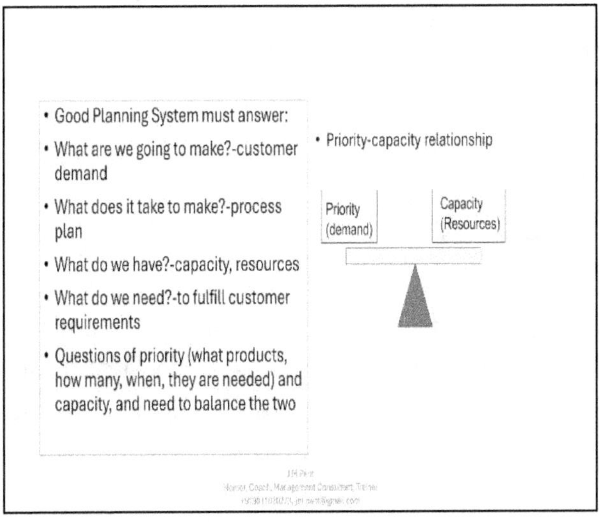

• Good Planning System must answer:
• What are we going to make?-customer demand
• What does it take to make?-process plan
• What do we have?-capacity, resources
• What do we need?-to fulfill customer requirements
• Questions of priority (what products, how many, when, they are needed) and capacity, and need to balance the two
• Priority-capacity relationship
Priority (demand)
Capacity (Resources)

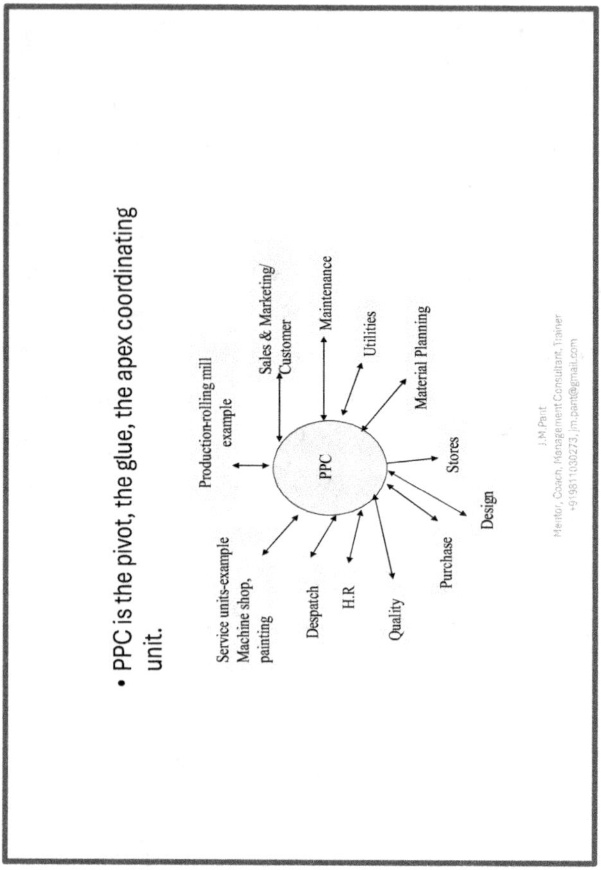
• PPC is the pivot, the glue, the apex coordinating unit.
PPC
Production-rolling mill example
Sales & Marketing/ Customer
Maintenance
Utilities
Material Planning
Stores
Design
Purchase
Quality
H.R
Despatch
Service units-example Machine shop, painting
J.M.Pant
Mentor, Coach, Management Consultant, Trainer
+919811030273, jm.pant@gmail.com

Steps in Production Planning
1.Demand Forecasting: Estimating future customer demand using historical data, market trends, and statistical methods.
2.Capacity Planning: Assessing the production

capacity needed to meet demand, considering factors like labour, machinery, and production time.
3.Resource Planning: Determining the materials, components, and other resources required..
4.Developing the Production Plan: Creating a detailed plan that outlines the production schedule, resources allocation, and timelines.

Production Scheduling

Production scheduling involves creating a detailed timetable for the production process, specifying when and where each task will be performed.

Types of Production Scheduling

1.***Master Production Schedule (MPS):*** A high-level plan that outlines what products will be produced, in what quantities, and when.
2.***Detailed Scheduling:*** Breaking down the MPS into specific tasks and assigning them to particular machines and workers.
3.***Dispatching*:** The process of assigning work orders to specific machines and operators at the right time..

Scheduling and Shop-Floor Decisions

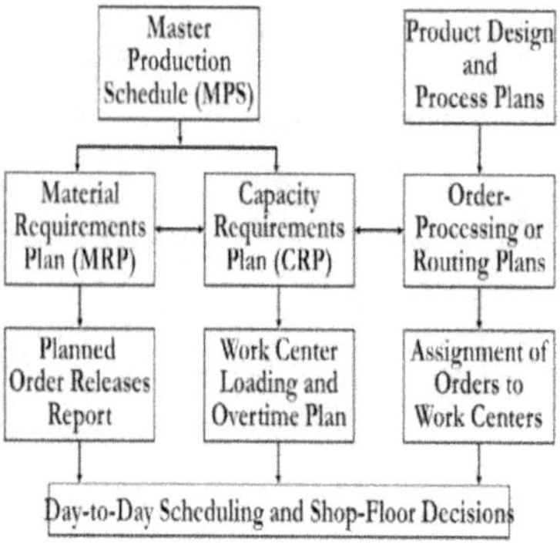
Master Production Schedule (MPS)
Product Design and Process Plans
Material Requirements Plan (MRP)
Capacity Requirements Plan (CRP)
Order-Processing or Routing Plans
Planned Order Releases Report
Work Center Loading and Overtime Plan
Assignment of Orders to Work Centers
Day-to-Day Scheduling and Shop-Floor Decisions

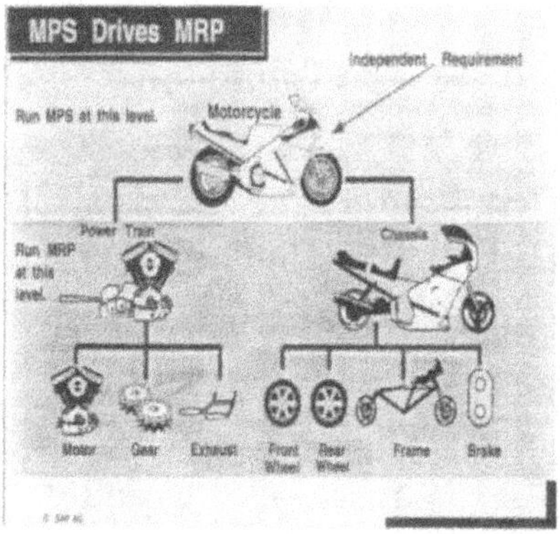
MPS Drives MRP
Independent Requirement
Run MPS at this level.
Motorcycle
Power Train
Chassis
Run MRP at this level.
Motor
Gear
Exhaust
Front Wheel
Rear Wheel
Frame
Brake

Techniques for Production Scheduling

1.***Gantt Charts***: Visual representation of the production schedule, showing the start and end times of tasks.
2.***PERT/CPM*** (Program Evaluation Review Technique/Critical Path Method): Tools for planning and controlling large projects, identifying the critical path and potential delays.
3.***Load Charts***: Display the workload of machines or work centers over time, helping to balance the load.

Production Control

Production control involves monitoring and adjusting the production process to ensure that the production plan is followed and objectives are met.

Functions of Production Control

1. ***Routing***: Determining the path that materials and components will follow through the production process.
2. ***Scheduling***: Establishing the timing and

sequence of operations.
3. ***Dispatching***: Issuing orders to start production activities.
4. ***Follow-Up and Expediting***: Monitoring the progress of production activities and making adjustments as needed.
5. ***Inspection***: Ensuring that the products meet quality standards through in-house Quality Control and Quality Assurance and second and third party inspection.
6. ***Inventory Control***: Managing inventory levels to ensure the availability of materials for continuity of production without overstocking.

Material Requirements Planning (MRP)

MRP is a systematic approach to planning and controlling inventory, production schedules, and procurement activities to ensure that materials are available for production and products are available for delivery to customers.

Objectives of MRP

1. ***Ensure Material Availability***: Making sure that the right materials are available at the right

time in quantity and quality for production.
2. ***Minimise Inventory Levels***: Reducing inventory costs by avoiding overstocking and understocking.
3. ***Improve Production Efficiency***: Streamlining production processes and reducing lead times.
4. ***Enhance Customer Service***: Ensuring timely delivery of finished products.

Components of MRP

1. Bill of Materials (BOM): A detailed list of all materials, components, and subassemblies required to produce a finished product.
2. Master Production Schedule (MPS): A plan for the production of finished goods, specifying what needs to be produced and when.
3. Inventory Records: Data on the current inventory levels, including quantities on hand, on order, and in transit.

MRP Process

1. Demand Forecasting: Estimating the future demand for finished products.
2. Exploding the BOM: Using the BOM to determine the quantities of each material and

component needed.

3. Netting: Calculating the net requirements for each item by subtracting the available inventory from the gross requirements.
4. Lot Sizing: Determining the quantities of items to be ordered or produced in each batch.
5. Scheduling: Establishing the timing of orders and production activities to meet the MPS.
6. Feedback and Adjustment: Continuously monitoring inventory levels, production progress, and demand changes, and making adjustments as necessary.

Benefits of MRP

1. Improved Inventory Management: More accurate and efficient control of inventory levels.
2. Enhanced Production Planning: Better coordination of production schedules and resources.
3. Increased Efficiency: Reduction in lead times and production delays.
4. Cost Savings: Lower inventory carrying costs and reduced waste.
5. Better Customer Service: Timely delivery of

products and improved order fulfilment.

Challenges in Production Planning, Scheduling, and Control

1. Demand Variability: Fluctuations in customer demand can make planning and scheduling difficult.

2. Complex Supply Chains: Coordinating with multiple suppliers and managing lead times can be challenging.

3. Resource Constraints: Limited availability of materials, labour, and machinery can impact production schedules.

4. Data Accuracy: Reliable data is crucial for effective planning and control, and inaccuracies can lead to issues.
5. Technological Integration: Integrating MRP

The most challenging PPC is in Job Manufacturing because of variety in jobs and in their manufacturing sequence, as well as variety in requirement of machine, manpower, resources and facilities.

Master Production Schedule- Monthly

Product		Apr	May	Jun	Jul	Aug	Sep	Oct	Nov	Dec	Jan	Feb	Mar
A													
B													
C													
D													
E													
Total													
Cumulative													

Master Production Schedule - Weekly

Prod	[illegible]
	[illegible]
A	
B	
C	
D	
E	
To	
Cu	

Production Schedule- Daily

	Week Total	April- Week 1						
Product		Day 1	Day 2	Day 3	Day 4	Day 5	Day 6	Weekly off
A								
B								
C								
D								
E								
Total								
Cumulative								

Production Schedule- Hourly

Product	Day Total	April- Week 1-day 1							
		Hr 1	Hr 2	Hr 3	Hr 4	Hr 5	Hr 6	Hr 7	Hr 8
A									
B									
C									
D									
E									
Total									
Cumulative									

Job cum Route Card

- **Job and Route Sheet/Card**

Ref.	JOB CARD AND ROUTE SHEET					Date
Component/Job. No.			Drawing No.			
Name of Job			Quantity			
Material			Delivery by		Plan	
					Actual	
Routing	Operation	Tools & Accessories		Set up time	Operation Time	Total time
Fabrication shop	Unit 1		Plan			
			Actual			
Machine shop	Nicholas		Plan			
			Actual			

Loading

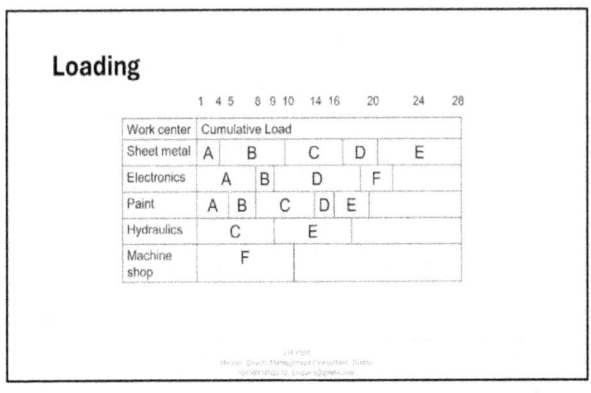

1 4 5 8 9 10 14 16 20 24 28

Work center	Cumulative Load
Sheet metal	A B C D E
Electronics	A B D F
Paint	A B C D E
Hydraulics	C E
Machine shop	F

Gantt Load Chart

- Shows relative work load in facility

Work centre	Mon	Tue	Wed	Thurs	Fri
Fabrication	Job 101	X		Job 350	
Machining		Job 111		Job 112	
Soldering	Job 301			Job 122	
Paint shop	Job 303			X	Job 306

X = Not available due to maintenance etc

☐ = Not scheduled

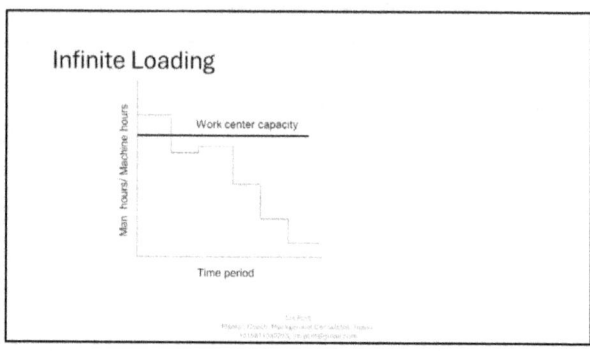

Infinite Loading

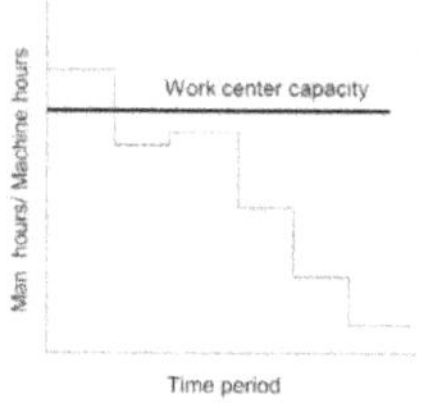

Work center capacity
Man hours/ Machine hours
Time period

Finite Loading

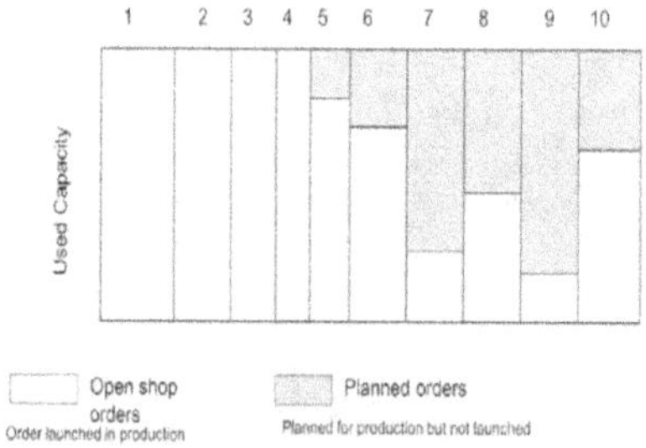

1 2 3 4 5 6 7 8 9 10
Used Capacity
Open shop orders
Order launched in production
Planned orders
Planned for production but not launched

Sequencing

Some sequencing rules (for setting priority of job processing)

- First come first served basis
- Earliest due date
- Shortest processing time
- Least slack (slack is defined as difference of time remaining from due date and length of its operation time)
- Critical ratio (CR): Time remaining until due date/processing time- Process lowest CR first
- Random order or whim.

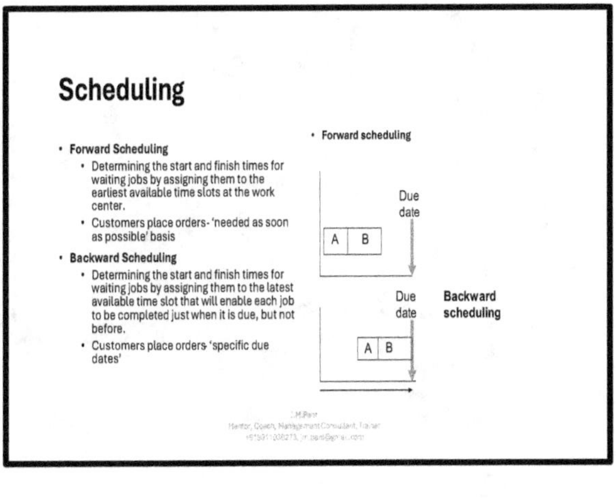

Scheduling
Forward Scheduling
Determining the start and finish times for waiting jobs by assigning them to the earliest available time slots at the work center.
Customers place orders- 'needed as soon as possible' basis
Backward Scheduling
Determining the start and finish times for waiting jobs by assigning them to the latest available time slot that will enable each job to be completed just when it is due, but not before.
Customers place orders- 'specific due dates'
Forward scheduling
Due date
A
B
Due date
A
B
Backward scheduling

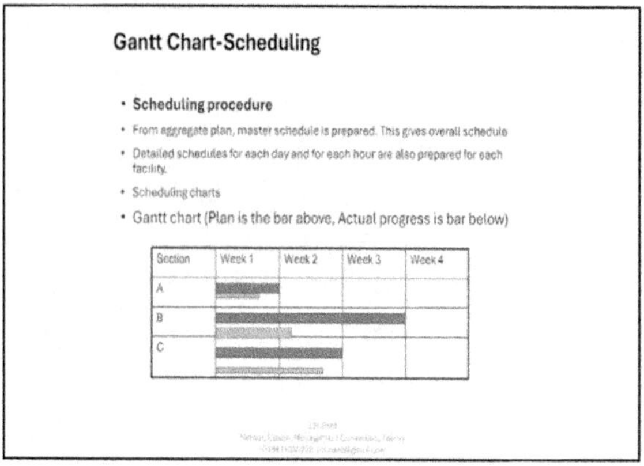
Gantt Chart-Scheduling
• Scheduling procedure
• From aggregate plan, master schedule is prepared. This gives overall schedule
• Detailed schedules for each day and for each hour are also prepared for each facility.
• Scheduling charts
• Gantt chart (Plan is the bar above, Actual progress is bar below)
Section
Week 1
Week 2
Week 3
Week 4
A
B
C

19
Kanban

Kanban is a scheduling system originally developed for lean manufacturing and just-in-time production. Over time, it has been adapted for various industries and is now widely used in operations management, providing a systematic approach to managing workflows and improving efficiency. By visualizing work, limiting WIP, and focusing on continuous improvement, Kanban helps operations teams deliver higher quality results, faster response times, and better resource utilization. Its adaptability makes it suitable for various operational contexts, from manufacturing to service delivery and project management.

Kanban, which means "signboard" or "billboard" in Japanese, was developed by Toyota in the late 1940s to improve manufacturing efficiency. The key principles of Kanban are to visualize work, limit work in progress (WIP), and enhance efficient workflow.

Kanban means a 'visible card.'
It is a method of controlling materials through a JIT manufacturing assembly by using cards to authorize a workstation to transfer or produce materials. No inventory is moved unless authorised by a 'move' card. Each bin contains a fixed, exact quantity of inventory, no more, no less. For each bin, there is exactly 1 Kanban card. As soon as materials are removed from a bin, the Kanban card is removed from the bin and placed in 'move' card box. If the bins are not removed by the subsequent process, the operator stops production.

Key Components of Kanban

1. Visual Signals: Kanban uses cards to represent work items. These cards move through different stages of a process on a Kanban board, which visualizes the flow of work and identifies bottlenecks.

2. Work-in-Progress (WIP) Limits: By limiting the number of tasks in each stage of the process, Kanban ensures that teams focus on completing work rather than starting new

tasks. This reduces multitasking and improves efficiency.

3. Flow Management: Continuous monitoring and managing of the flow of work help in identifying and resolving inefficiencies.

4. Continuous Improvement (Kaizen): Kanban encourages teams to continuously look for ways to improve processes. Regular reviews and adjustments help in optimizing operations.

Application in Operations Management

1.Production and Inventory Control: Kanban is used to manage inventory levels by signalling when to reorder materials, thus minimising overproduction and excess inventory. It ensures that the right amount of resources is available at the right time.

2. Project Management: In operations management, Kanban boards help in planning, tracking, and managing projects. Tasks are visualized on the board, providing a clear overview of the project status and helping teams to stay on track.

3. Service Management: For service operations, Kanban helps in managing service requests, incident responses, and other workflows. It ensures that services are delivered efficiently and within the expected time frames.

4. Supply Chain Management: Kanban systems facilitate just-in-time delivery in the supply chain, reducing waste and improving responsiveness to demand changes. It aligns production schedules with actual consumption patterns.

Implementation Steps

1. ***Map the Current Process***: Identify and visualize the existing workflow on a Kanban board. Define the stages that work items pass through.
2. ***Create Kanban Cards***: Represent work items with Kanban cards. Include relevant information such as task description, assignee, and due date.
3. ***Set WIP Limits***: Establish limits for the number of tasks that can be in progress at each stage. Adjust these limits based on team capacity and workload.

4. ***Monitor and Adapt*:** Review the flow of work, identify bottlenecks, and make necessary adjustments. Use metrics such as cycle time and throughput to measure performance.

5.***Foster a Culture of Continuous Improvement*:** Encourage teams to suggest and implement improvements. Conduct regular retrospectives to discuss what is working well and what can be improved.

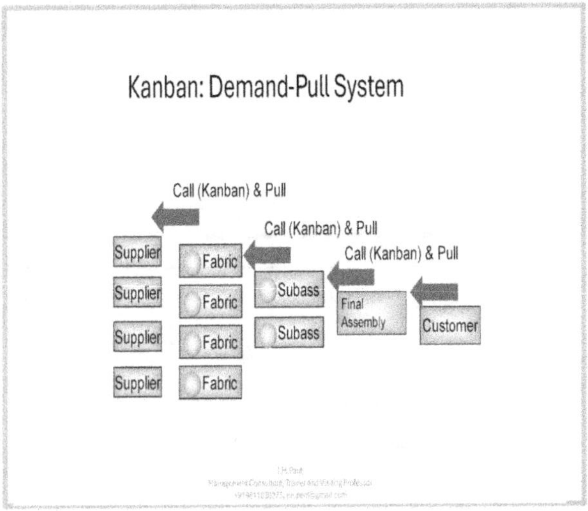
Kanban: Demand-Pull System
Call (Kanban) & Pull
Call (Kanban) & Pull
Call (Kanban) & Pull
Supplier
Supplier
Supplier
Supplier
Fabric
Fabric
Fabric
Fabric
Subass
Subass
Final Assembly
Customer

Conveyance Kanban

Part number to produce: **M471-36** | **Part description:** **Valve Housing**

Lot size needed: 40 | **Container type: RED Crate**

Card number: 2/ 5 | **Retrieval storage location: N3**

From work center: 22 | **To work center: 35**

Number of Kanbans N:

$N = [DL(1+\alpha)]/A$

Where

D=demand per unit of time

L=lead time

A =container capacity

α= safety stock factor

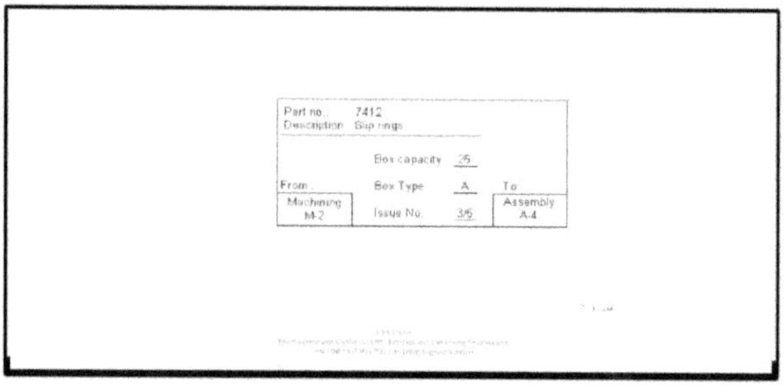
Part no.: 7412
Description: Slip rings
Box capacity 25
From: Machining M-2
Box Type A
To: Assembly A-4
Issue No. 3/5

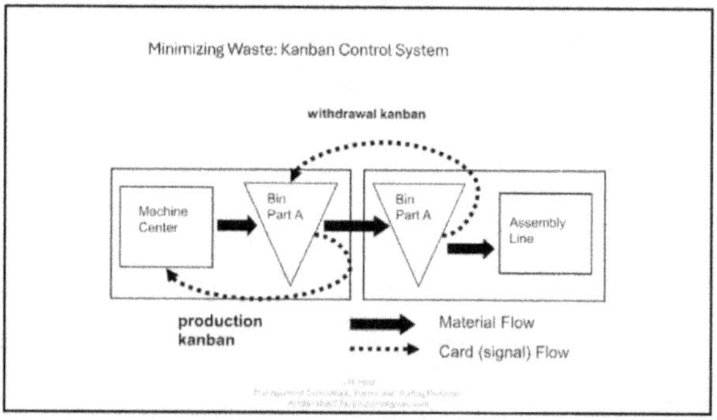
Minimizing Waste: Kanban Control System
withdrawal kanban
Machine Center
Bin Part A
Bin Part A
Assembly Line
production kanban
Material Flow
Card (signal) Flow

Move 'Kanban'

Example

- A switch is assembled in batches of 4 units at an "upstream" work area.
- delivered in a bin to a "downstream" control-panel assembly area that requires 5 switch assemblies/hour.
- The switch assembly area can produce a bin of switch assemblies in 2 hours.
- Safety stock = 10% of needed inventory.

$$k = \frac{\text{Expected demand during lead time + safety stock}}{\text{size of container}}$$

$$= \frac{dL(1+S)}{C} = \frac{5(2)(1.1)}{4} = 2.75 \text{ or } 3$$

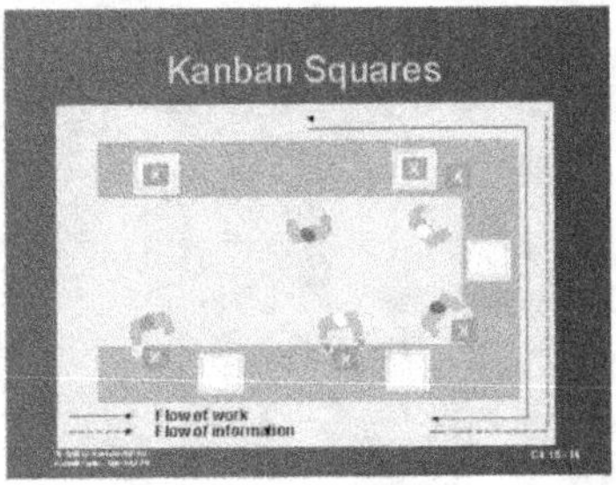
Kanban Squares
Flow of work
Flow of information

Examples of Containers and Kanban Signals

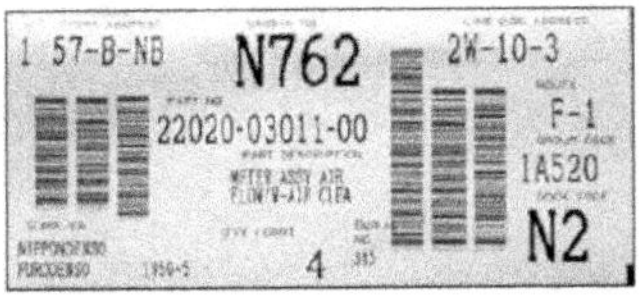
1 57-B-NB
N762
2W-10-3
22020-03011-00
F-1
1A520
N2
4

20
JIT

Imagine you're cooking a big dinner for friends. You want everything to be hot and fresh when they arrive, so you don't start cooking until the last possible moment. But what if you don't have enough ingredients? Or what if you start too late and end up serving dinner at midnight? That's the delicate dance of Just-In-Time (JIT) in Operations Management – making sure everything is ready exactly when it's needed, not too early and not too late.

The Basics of JIT

JIT is a strategy and a management philosophy used in manufacturing and other industries to increase efficiency by exposing problems and bottlenecks by taking away the security blanket, and reduce waste by receiving goods only as they are needed in the production process. This means materials arrive just in time for their use, not sitting around taking up space.

JIT is a 'PULL' system for high-volume production as per demand with minimal inventory (raw materials, WIP, finished goods), and involves timed arrivals at the workstation, unlike the conventional 'PUSH' system where production goes as per plan leading to inventories if the subsequent station is not ready to receive the material or there is no demand. JIT reduces 'buffer' stocks and forces one to identify waste in the production system and eliminate or reduce them for smoother production run.

The Essence of JIT

To put it simply, JIT is like trying to make it to the airport exactly on time for your flight – not so early that you're bored out of your mind, and not so late that you're sprinting through the terminal. You want to get there, get on the plane, and go.

JIT requires ① employee participation, ② smaller lots, batch and order sizes, ③ faster set ups and reduced die, tool and other changeovers, ④ reduced lead times and frequent deliveries, reliable suppliers and consistency in supply times, ⑤ continuous improvement and reduction of all types of wastes like defects and rework, idling of equipment and people, breakdowns, excess transport and movement and motions due to poor layout, unnecessary processing, bad method of working, inventories in stores, in transit and conveyors, line and capacity imbalance, and others.

On a lighter note

My school friend Dhruv Chak has got this knack for always finishing Wordle in exactly six tries, which is the allowable limit. Dhruv likes to joke that it's his version of JIT – finishing just in time, every time. It's like he's perfected the art of doing just enough to get the job done, right when it's needed. He never stresses out on the first few tries – he's calm, collected, and always seems to get it done just in time. It's like he's saying, "Why rush? I'll get it done when it needs to be done."

How JIT Works in Real Life

Let's take a closer look at how JIT works in the real world with some relatable examples:

Example 1: Car Manufacturing

Imagine a car factory. Instead of storing piles of car parts in a warehouse, the factory orders parts to arrive just as they are needed on the assembly line. So, if the factory needs 100 tyres on Monday, those tyres are delivered Monday morning, not weeks in advance. This reduces storage costs and waste.

One of the lines for a renowned car manufacturer in India, which had 11 machines and 2 operators, had historically taken 6 hours for set up change. After making improvements like SMED (Single minute exchange of dies) and others, and using a cross-functional teams, the car maker slashed set up time to 20 minutes.

JIT based deliveries-An efficient ancillary to a car manufacturer in Gurgaon makes 16 deliveries a day to the parent unit which takes the items to its line directly trusting the vendor's quality, and thereby not keeping any inventory of the parts of the vendor.
Low cost automation, machine lay out changes, mistake proofing of critical processes and

better segregation of sub-assemblies enabled it to be a world class supplier.

Example 2: Your Favourite Café

Think about your favourite café. They don't bake hundreds of pastries at the start of the day and hope they sell. Instead, they bake in smaller batches throughout the day, ensuring that pastries are fresh and there's minimal waste. If they run out, they can quickly bake more. This is a JIT approach to inventory.

Benefits of JIT

- ***Reduced Inventory Costs***: By only having what you need, when you need it, you don't spend money storing excess inventory.
- ***Less Waste***: Perishable goods don't go bad, and there's less likelihood of products becoming obsolete.
- ***Increased Efficiency***: Production processes are streamlined, and workers are always working on current tasks, not trying to manage piles of extra materials.

Challenges of JIT

Of course, JIT isn't without its challenges. What happens if the delivery truck gets stuck in traffic? Suddenly, your assembly line is halted because you don't have the parts you need. JIT requires excellent coordination and reliable suppliers.

JIT in Your Daily Life

You might already be using JIT principles without realizing it. Ever gone grocery shopping with a list of exactly what you need for the week? That's JIT shopping. You're not buying a year's worth of canned beans, just what you need for your meals this week. It saves you from wasting food and keeps your pantry from overflowing.

JIT

21
Supply Chain Management

Supply Chain Management (SCM) starts and ends with customer and involves the coordination and management of a network of interconnected businesses involved in providing goods and services to end customers. Supply chain management is a set of approaches used to efficiently integrate suppliers, manufacturers, warehouses, and customers so that merchandise is produced and distributed at the right quantities, to the right locations, and at the right time in order to minimise system wide costs while satisfying service-level requirements.

SCM encompasses the planning and management of all activities involved in sourcing, procurement, conversion, and logistics management. Additionally, it includes coordination and collaboration with channel partners, which can be suppliers, intermediaries, third-party service providers, and customers.

Supply Chain is the sequence of organisations - their facilities, warehouses, factories, processing centers, distribution centers, retail outlets, functions, and activities – from getting customer requirement, designing, procuring materials, inbound logistics, storage and inventory, producing, quality check, dispatching and outbound logistics for delivery to customer of the product or service. It is a **value chain,** and lot of money can be saved through effective and efficient management of the value chain. All functions should be done well integrating all the activities in the value chain.

It may seem to many as an unglamorous job of overseeing the movement of goods from the customer's order through to production, storage, and distribution. Supply chain managers often make the difference between happy customers and irate ones, and in today's cost-conscious times, they're more valuable than ever. Organisations are under tremendous pressure to cut costs, and most of those costs are just sitting there in the supply chain.
SCM functions and activities includes, among other things, forecasting, purchasing, inventory

management, information management, ERP, QA, Scheduling, Production and Delivery, and Customer service.

SCM tries to achieve balance between three conflicting goals of low inventory, low operation cost and high service level, through integration of purchase, operations and distribution systems.

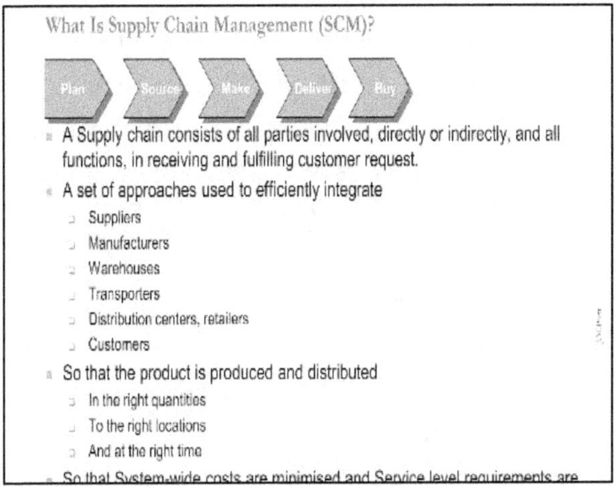

What Is Supply Chain Management (SCM)?
Plan
Source
Make
Deliver
Buy
A Supply chain consists of all parties involved, directly or indirectly, and all functions, in receiving and fulfilling customer request.
A set of approaches used to efficiently integrate
Suppliers
Manufacturers
Warehouses
Transporters
Distribution centers, retailers
Customers
So that the product is produced and distributed
In the right quantities
To the right locations
And at the right time

So that System-wide costs are minimised and Service level requirements are satisfied.

Supply Chain Performance Drivers

①Quality, ②Cost, ③Lead time, ④Velocity, ⑤Flexibility, ⑥Customer Service.

Quality of product and service, including customer service, throughout the supply chain for full customer satisfaction and delight.

Cost reduction at every segment of supply chain. Inventory is one critical component of Cost which should be minimised.

Lead Time: Reduce lead time to derive a competitive edge, increase throughput and cash flow resulting in higher ROI. This includes Product Development (Design) Lead Time, Purchasing (including Sourcing) Lead Time, Manufacturing (Production) Lead Time, Queue time before processing, Set up time, Run (processing) time, Waiting time after processing, Move time, Order Processing Lead Time, Distribution Lead Time, Others (e.g. decision making, coordination) Lead Time.

Flexibility of Manpower, of Equipment, of work timings, of layout, of process. Flexibility increases agility and adaptability to Change. Rigidity constraints us and enables competitors to outmanoeuvre us.

Customer Service implies quick response, and meeting commitments using the golden principle of under promise and over deliver, so that repeat business and customer referrals will be easier.

1.MRP

Material Requirement Plan (MRP) is a system used to avoid material shortages and missing parts. MRP establishes a schedule showing when the material is required based on the Master Production Schedule (MPS) requirements. Based on lead times, and inventory available, MRP calculates the quantity and the time in which the order must be placed.

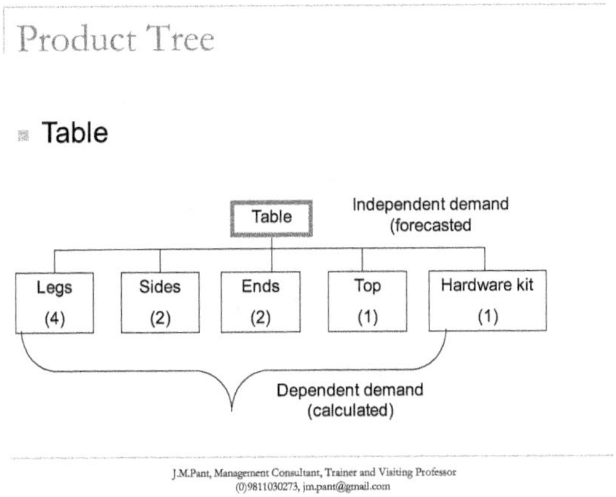
Product Tree
Table
Table
Independent demand
(forecasted
Legs
(4)
Sides
(2)
Ends
(2)
Top
(1)
Hardware kit
(1)
Dependent demand
(calculated)
J.M.Pant, Management Consultant, Trainer and Visiting Professor
(0)9811030273, jm.pant@gmail.com

Materials Planning

- Material Plan

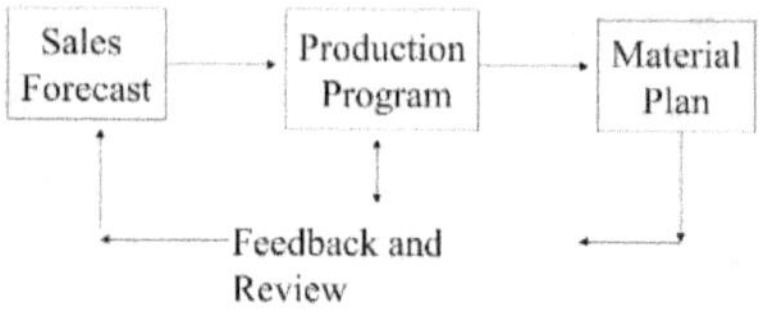
Sales Forecast
Production Program
Material Plan
Feedback and Review

J M Pant, Management Consultant, Trainer and Visiting Professor
(91)9811030273, jm.pant@gmail.com

Materials Planning

- Material Plan

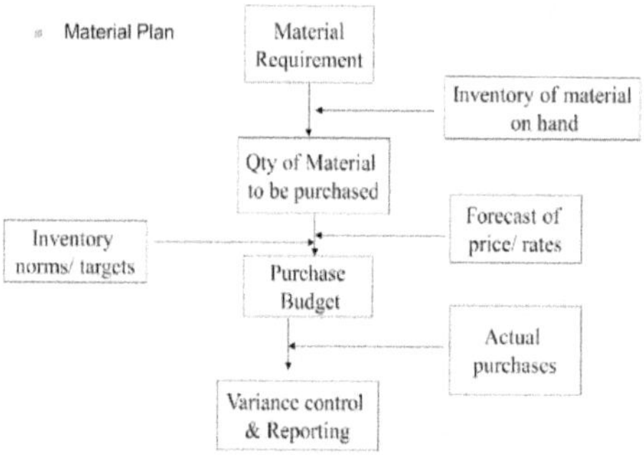
Material Requirement
Inventory of material on hand
Qty of Material to be purchased
Forecast of price/ rates
Inventory norms/ targets
Purchase Budget
Actual purchases
Variance control & Reporting

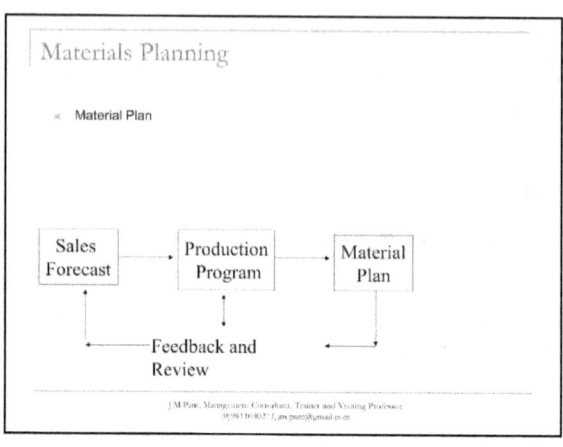

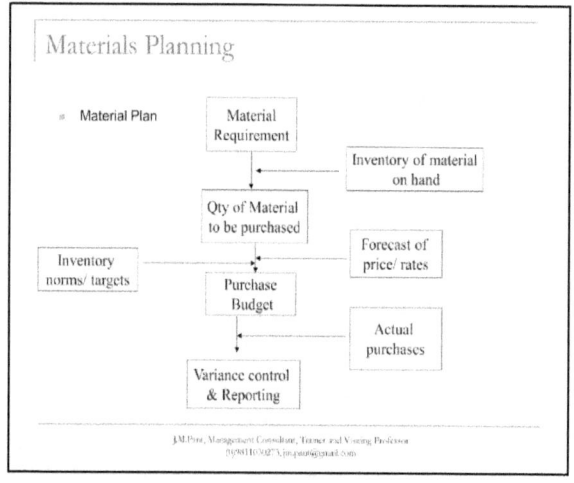

J.M.Pant, Management Consultant, Trainer and Visiting Professor
(91)9811030273, jm.pant@gmail.com

Bill of Materials (BOM)

A Bill of Materials (BOM) is a comprehensive list of raw materials, components, subassemblies, and quantities needed to manufacture a finished product. Serving as a central reference, the BOM outlines every item required in the production process, from the smallest screw to the main assembly. It functions like a recipe for manufacturing, detailing the necessary parts and their relationships, ensuring that all required materials are available at the right time and in the right quantities. This essential document helps streamline procurement, inventory management, and production planning, reducing errors, minimizing waste, and ensuring efficient workflow. One needs to maintain an accurate and up-to-date BOM.

The BOM example shows that for 1 unit of chair one needs 2.7 units of fabric, or for 100 units of chair, 270 units of fabric are required. The techniques for estimating material requirements are: 1. Sales Forecasting, 2. Past consumption analysis, and 3. Bill of materials explosion.

<Example BOM-Bill of Materials>

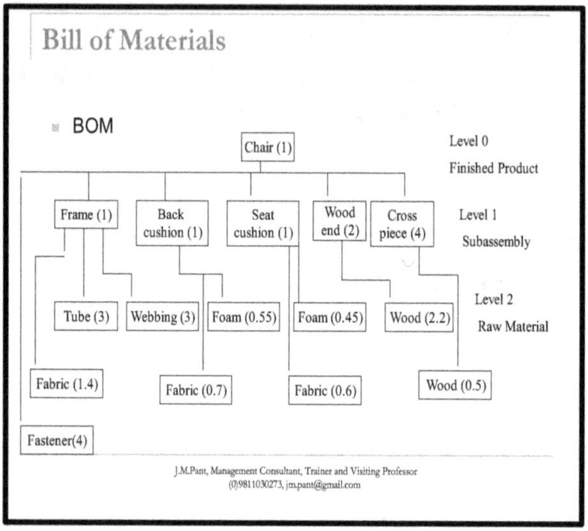

Bill of Materials
BOM
Chair (1)
Level 0
Finished Product
Frame (1)
Back cushion (1)
Seat cushion (1)
Wood end (2)
Cross piece (4)
Level 1
Subassembly
Tube (3)
Webbing (3)
Foam (0.55)
Foam (0.45)
Wood (2.2)
Level 2
Raw Material
Fabric (1.4)
Fabric (0.7)
Fabric (0.6)
Wood (0.5)
Fastener(4)
J.M.Pant, Management Consultant, Trainer and Visiting Professor
(0)9811030273, jm.pant@gmail.com

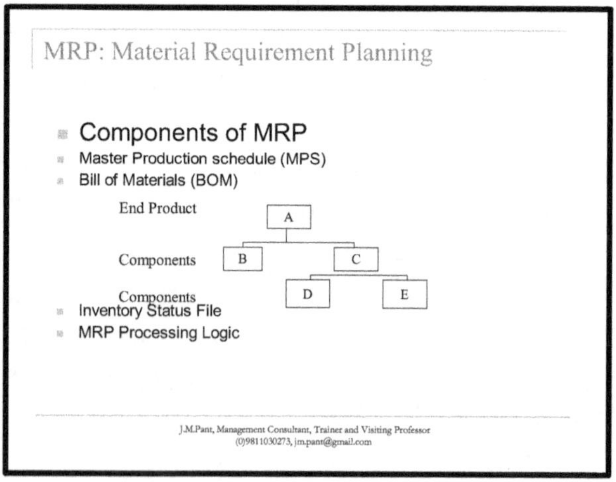

MRP: Material Requirement Planning
Components of MRP
Master Production schedule (MPS)
Bill of Materials (BOM)
End Product
A
Components
B
C
Components
D
E
Inventory Status File
MRP Processing Logic
J.M.Pant, Management Consultant, Trainer and Visiting Professor
(0)9811030273, jm.pant@gmail.com

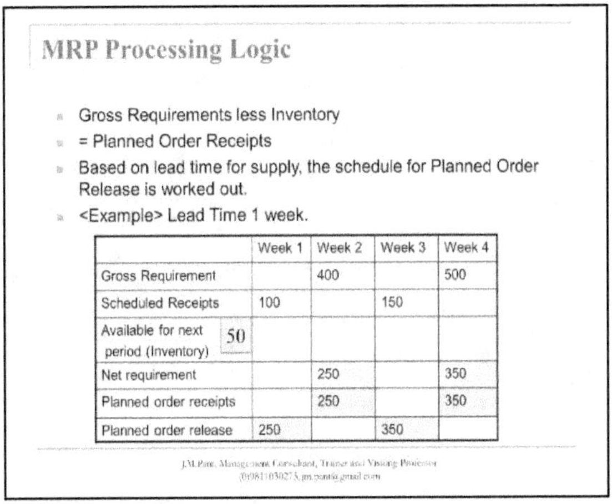

MRP Processing Logic

- Gross Requirements less Inventory
- = Planned Order Receipts
- Based on lead time for supply, the schedule for Planned Order Release is worked out.
- <Example> Lead Time 1 week.

	Week 1	Week 2	Week 3	Week 4
Gross Requirement		400		500
Scheduled Receipts	100		150	
Available for next period (Inventory) 50				
Net requirement		250		350
Planned order receipts		250		350
Planned order release	250		350	

2.Inventory Management

Inventory management is the process of ordering, storing, and using a company's inventory. This includes the management of raw materials, components, supplies, work in progress and finished products, maintenance spares and consumables, as well as warehousing and processing such items.

Inventory is a Waste. Inventory is Non Value adding in most cases (exceptions where storage adds value like wine). Inventory has to be optimised. More Inventory adds to cost, while less Inventory may result in stock-out, and poor customer service and therefore the need to balance the two extremes.

Why Inventory Management?

- To meet demand; random demand variations, seasonal demand; better customer service.
- To smooth operations, have uninterrupted flow.
- To decouple operations, create buffer.
- To prevent stockouts (missed delivery, lost sales, dissatisfied customer, production loss).
- To prevent overstock (blocked capital, opportunity loss)
- To hedge against price increases.
- To take advantage of quantity discounts and economic lot size in purchase and operations.

Inventory Counting System

Periodic System: Physical count of items made at periodic intervals.

Perpetual Inventory System: System that keeps track of removals from inventory continuously, thus monitoring current levels of each item.

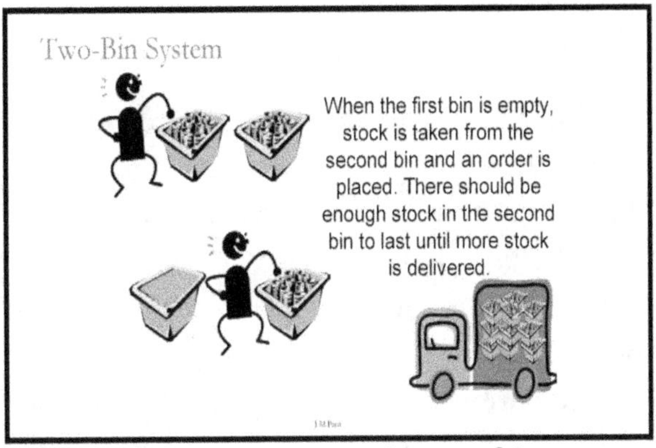
Two-Bin System
When the first bin is empty, stock is taken from the second bin and an order is placed. There should be enough stock in the second bin to last until more stock is delivered.

Two-Bin System: Two containers of inventory; reorder when the first is empty.

Universal Bar Code: Bar code printed on a label that has information about the item to which it is attached.

0 214800 232087768

Inventory Management Techniques

- ***Just-In-Time (JIT)***: Inventory strategy where materials are ordered and received only as they are needed in the production process.
- ***Economic Order Quantity (EOQ)***: The ideal order quantity a company should purchase to minimise inventory costs such as carrying or holding costs, shortage or stockout

costs, and ordering costs.

- *ABC Analysis*: Inventory categorisation method that divides items into three categories (A, B, and C) based on their importance and value. This based on 20:80 rule or Pareto principle that a vital few (20%) make up most (80%) of inventory.

A items are the most valuable, representing a small percentage of the total number of items but a large percentage of the total inventory value. These items require focus and high-priority management, frequent reordering, and close monitoring.

<Example> Expensive components or raw materials essential to production.

B items fall in between A and C categories, representing a moderate percentage of both total items and inventory value. The emphasis is on moderate management effort and periodic reordering.

<Example> Mid-range priced items that are important but not as critical as A items.

C items are trivial many representing a large percentage of the total number of items but a small percentage of the total inventory value.

They fall in low-priority management, bulk ordering, and less frequent reordering.
<Example>Low-cost, high-quantity items like screws, bolts, or stationery.

Similar to ABC method of Selective Inventory Control are classification FSN-Fast moving, Slow moving and Non Moving Stocks which is useful in prioritising SKUs in terms of their movement or consumption. Also prioritising based on Procurement are VED-Vital or critical to production and must always be in stock, Essential items which are important but not critical, and moderate stock, Desirable to keep but minimal as they are easy to procure. Another prioritisation based on Value of items is HML-High cost, Medium cost and Low cost.

- ***Safety Stock***: Additional quantity of an item held in the inventory to reduce the risk of stockouts.

Optimising Inventory- EOQ

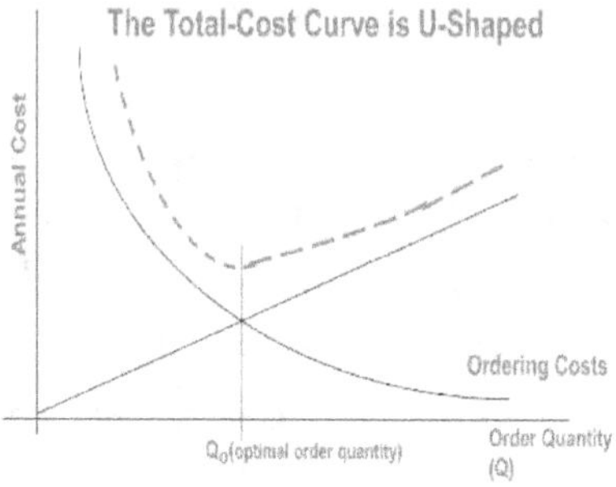

The Total-Cost Curve is U-Shaped
Annual Cost
Ordering Costs
Q0(optimal order quantity)
Order Quantity (Q)

Adding Value To Supply Chain: Optimising Inventory Level

- Inventory Model

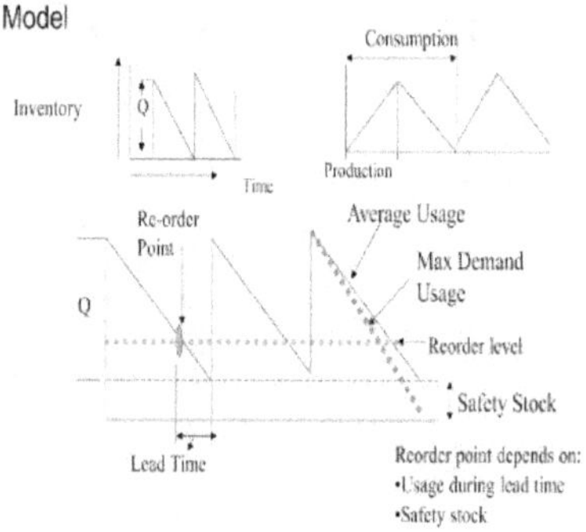

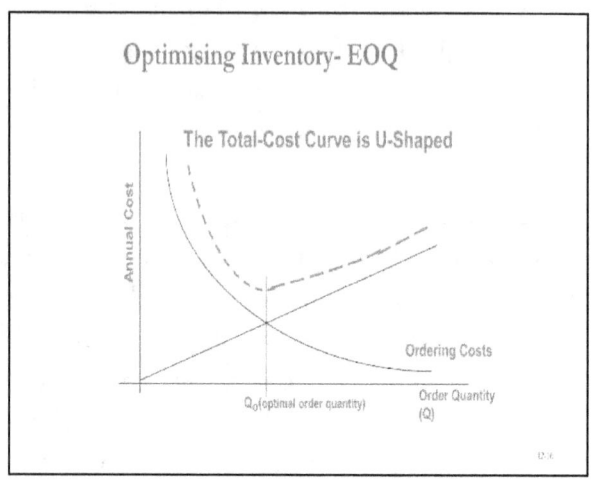

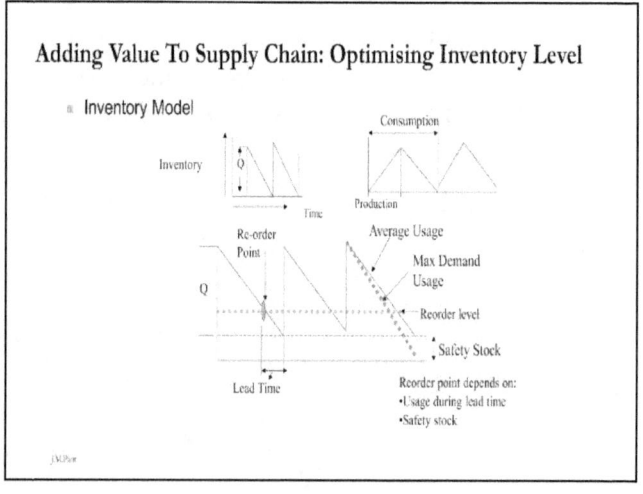

Consumption
Inventory
Q
Time
Production
Re-order Point
Average Usage
Max Demand Usage
Q
Reorder level
Safety Stock
Lead Time
Reorder point depends on:
•Usage during lead time
•Safety stock

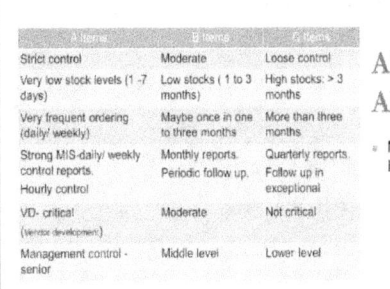

A Items	B Items	C Items
Strict control	Moderate	Loose control
Very low stock levels (1 -7 days)	Low stocks (1 to 3 months)	High stocks: > 3 months
Very frequent ordering (daily/ weekly)	Maybe once in one to three months	More than three months
Strong MIS-daily/ weekly control reports. Hourly control	Monthly reports. Periodic follow up.	Quarterly reports. Follow up in exceptional
VD- critical (vendor development)	Moderate	Not critical
Management control - senior	Middle level	Lower level

ABC ANALYSIS

- Managerial Intervention

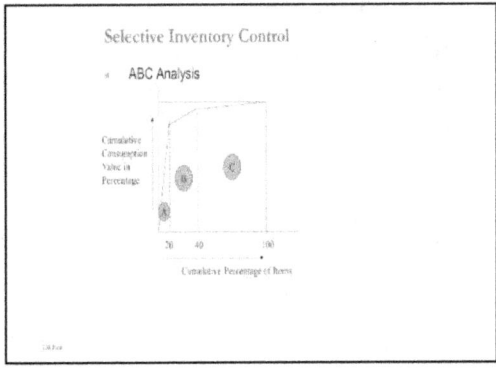

Selective Inventory Control

- ABC Analysis

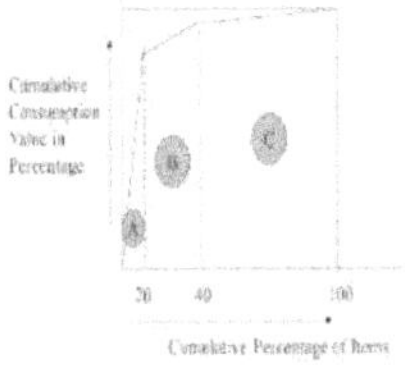
Cumulative Consumption Value in Percentage
A
B
C
20
40
100
Cumulative Percentage of Items

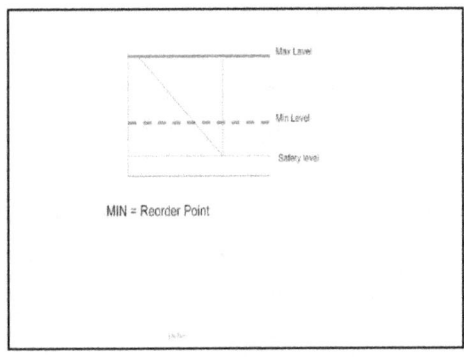

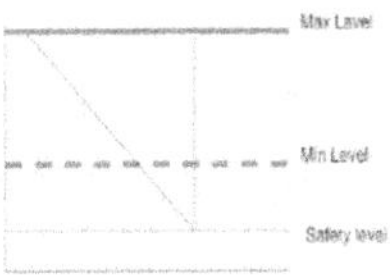
Max Level
Min Level
Safety level

MIN = Reorder Point

Reduce Inventory Cost

***1.Reduce Carrying cost*:**

Reduce lot size and increase frequency of supplies.

Reduce lead time and variation.

Improve demand forecasting.

Reduce bank financial charges.

Reduce insurance percentage.

Reduce pilferage, theft, obsolescence.

Reduce warehousing cost.

Reduce material cost.

Reduce wastage-spillage, deterioration, scrap.

Reduce stock outs,

***2.Reduce Ordering cost*:**

Purchase dept. cost, manpower.

Paperwork to paperless; digital.

Process improvement-indenting, approval, ordering, e-bidding, e-auction, intranet for internal approvals etc.

***3.Reduce Purchasing cost*:**

Negotiation with suppliers, transporters to reduce cost.

Make correct procurement specifications

Get Quality suppliers, right source.

Effective tendering process, go global.

Credit from suppliers; extended payment terms
Supplier discounts-volume, relationship building.

4.Reducing Lead Time – Internal

Reduce time from purchase need of user to indent

Eliminate delay because of procedures, because of incomplete information and specifications, design details, samples etc.

Reduce time for approval of indent, eliminate delay because of file movement.

Reduce time to float enquiries/ tendering process, reduce delay because of mode of enquiry

Reduce delays by tendering committee and tendering process:

- Time waits for receiving tenders.
- Time for opening of tenders.
- Time for preparing comparative chart.
- Time for evaluation of offers.
- Time for negotiation of offers.
- Time for preparing purchase order
- Time for sanction of Purchase Order.
- Time for release/despatch of purchase order to supplier.

- In all places, reduce wait time, queue time, move time, set up time, run time.

5.Reducing Lead Time – External

Reducing suppliers' lead time for manufacturing and/or preparing/fulfilling the order by managing Overload at suppliers' unit. Prioritizing and creating sense of urgency, scheduling buyer's order in plan of supplier,
Resolving supplier Quality, Process, Equipment, engineering or manpower, IR problems resulting in delays, reducing time for buyers' QC check at supplier end, reducing time for transport from supplier unit to buyer unit/freight time.

6.Reducing Lead Time – Internal (after receipt of material in stores)

Reducing time wait for QC inspection and clearance.

3. Purchasing Management

Purchasing management involves the process of acquiring goods and services for business use. It includes the sourcing, negotiating, and buying of materials needed for production and operation. The purchasing process starts with need identification for materials, supplier selection for that material, from the host of suppliers in database, based on quality, price, availability and reliability. Once the suppliers are short listed, they are given enquiries with complete specifications and sample or details of item needed including drawing where necessary.

-Purchase Requisition PR or indent: The authorised user initiates the requirement along with specifications, sample, drawings.

-Enquiry or Tender: Based on PR, tender enquiries are floated-limited to few or open tender soliciting proposals based on the specifications.

-Shortlisting and negotiations based on technical criteria first, and the ones filtered after fulfilling technical requirements, are scrutinised for price bids and the supplier is selected based on criteria decided by the Evaluation Committee.

- Purchase Order (PO): Formal request for the supply of products or services.
- Order Receipt and Quality check/Inspection:

Receiving and verifying the products ordered.(GRN-Goods Receipt Note or similar format)
- Invoice Approval and Payment: Authorising and making payment for the received goods.

Supplier Relationship Management
Maintaining good relationships with suppliers is crucial for ensuring the timely delivery of goods, obtaining the best prices, and ensuring quality.

4. Stores Management

Stores management is the process of managing the storage of goods and materials. It involves receiving, storing, and issuing materials as needed.

Store Layout and Design
Efficient store layout and design are crucial for effective stores management. This includes the arrangement of racks, shelves, and bins to maximise space utilization and streamline the movement of goods.

Stock or Inventory Control

- ***Perpetual Inventory System***: Continuously updating the inventory records.
- ***Periodic Inventory System***: Updating inventory records at regular intervals.
- ***Stock Verification***: Regular checks to ensure physical stock matches the inventory records.

SKUs

Reduce the number of Stock Keeping Units (SKUs) which will help in inventory control and efficient management. <Example> Tiles of different sizes/ styles/colurs/ design/material would be different SKUs.

Lot Size Decision Rules

Min-Max system

Order when quantity falls below re-order point.

Order Quantity =Max level – actual stock

Minimum Quantity Level = (Average lead time in days X Average daily demand) + Safety stock.

EOQ (Economic Order Quantity)

Two Bin System

Economic Lot Size of Vendor

Indent based

MRP based

Period-order quantity system< Order 'n' periods supply; Fixed Order interval. Order Qty to cover future periods requirement.

Storage Techniques

- *First-In-First-Out (FIFO)*: Method where the oldest inventory items are used first.
- *Last-In-First-Out (LIFO):* Method where the most recently produced items are used first.
- *Batch Control*: Managing inventory based on production or purchase batches.

5. Logistics Management

Logistics management involves planning, implementing, and controlling the efficient flow and storage of goods, services, and related information from the point of origin to the point of consumption; both inbound logistics-from source/supplier of material to plant and outbound logistics-from plant to customer.

Components of Logistics Management

- **Transportation**: Movement of goods from one location to another. Modes include road,

rail, air, and sea. It involves freight management, optimising cost, carrier (or transportation provider) selection based on cost, reliability, service quality; route planning.
- **Warehousing**: Storage of goods until they are needed. Decisions on Centralised warehousing consolidating inventory in a single location; Decentralised warehousing distributing inventory over multiple locations; and Cross docking which is minimising storage by directly transferring incoming goods to outgoing transport requiring synchronisation.
- **Distribution Management**: Ensuring products reach the end customer in the most efficient and effective manner.
- **Logistics Information Systems** Technologies used to plan and control logistics activities.

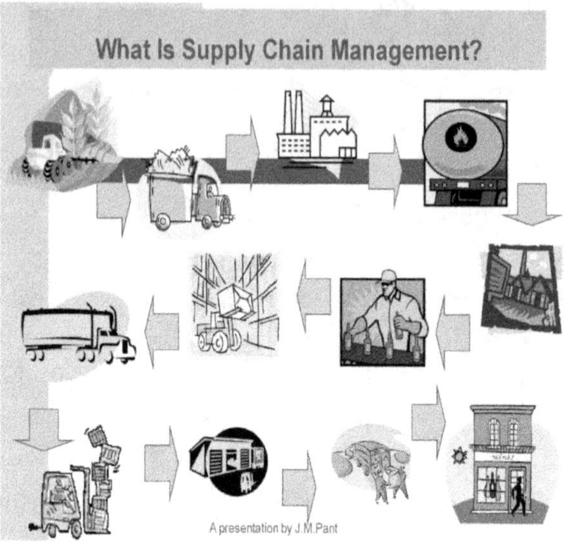
What Is Supply Chain Management?
A presentation by J.M.Pant

What Is Supply Chain Management?

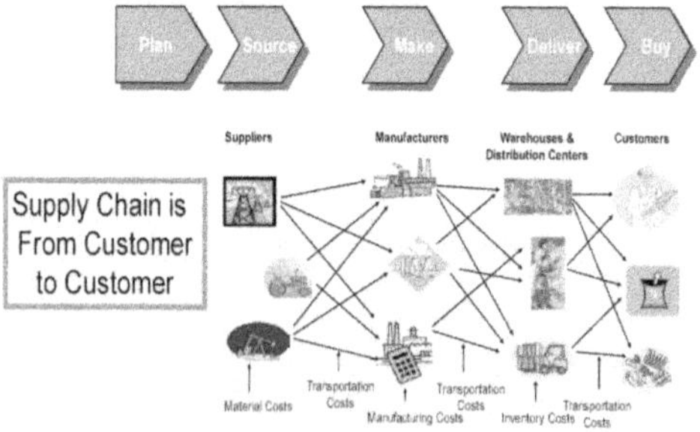
Plan
Source
Make
Deliver
Buy
Suppliers
Manufacturers
Warehouses & Distribution Centers
Customers
Supply Chain is From Customer to Customer
Material Costs
Transportation Costs
Manufacturing Costs
Transportation Costs
Inventory Costs
Transportation Costs

J.M.Pant

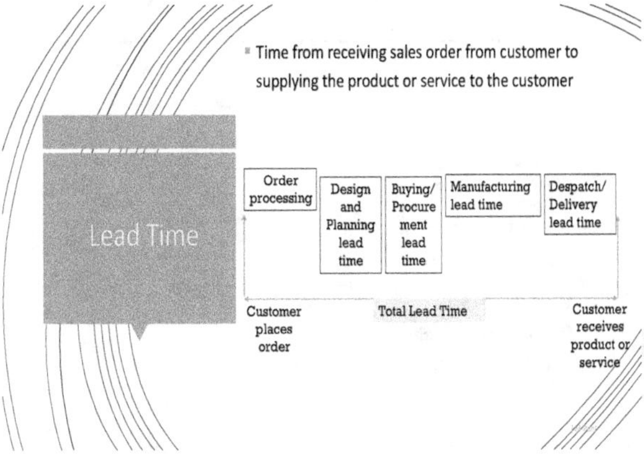
Time from receiving sales order from customer to supplying the product or service to the customer
Lead Time
Order processing
Design and Planning lead time
Buying/ Procurement lead time
Manufacturing lead time
Despatch/ Delivery lead time
Customer places order
Total Lead Time
Customer receives product or service

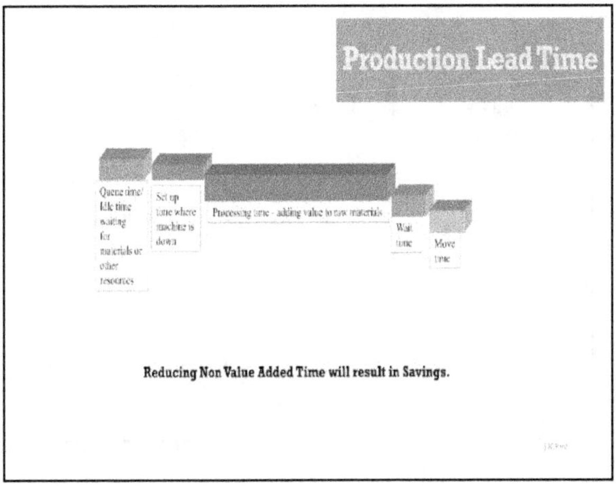
Production Lead Time
Queue time/ Idle time waiting for materials or other resources
Set up time where machine is down
Processing time - adding value to raw materials
Wait time
Move time
Reducing Non Value Added Time will result in Savings.

Supply Chain Performance Drivers

- Velocity
  - Volume of sales
  - Speed of work
- Rate of rotation of working capital
- Inventory velocity
  - The rate at which inventory(material) goes through the supply chain.
- Information velocity
  - The rate at which information is communicated in a supply chain.

Quality
Cost
Lead time
Flexibility
Velocity
Customer
Service

Velocity Improves Cash To Cash Cycle

- The faster the rotation, greater will be ROI. Disruptions/Stoppages, long routes, low speed, delays will reduce ROI.

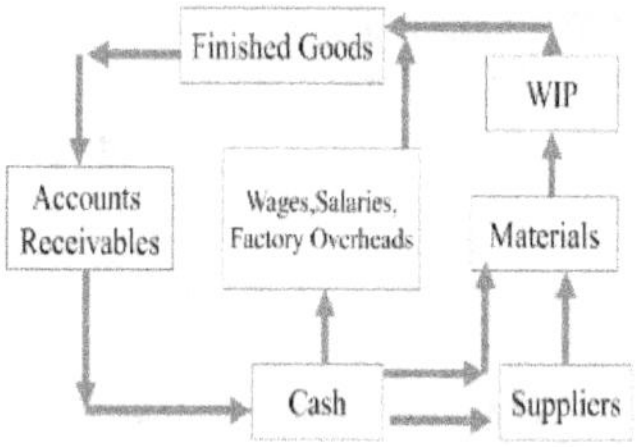

Finished Goods
WIP
Accounts Receivables
Wages,Salaries, Factory Overheads
Materials
Cash
Suppliers

22

Industrial Engineering- Job Design, Work Study, Value Engineering

Industrial engineering and work study are critical areas within operations management, focusing on improving efficiency, productivity, and quality in manufacturing and service industries. Industrial engineering deals with the optimisation of complex systems, including equipment design, layout, supply chain, inventory, operations research, and simulation models, while work study involves the systematic examination of tasks and processes to identify and eliminate inefficiencies.

Job analysis involves the systematic study of components of a job with a view to improve the method or process of doing a job, measuring the work content of a job in terms of time, and organising roles and responsibilities, identifying necessary skills, and the conditions under which the jobs are to be performed. This helps in recruitment, training, performance appraisal, and job design.

The smallest component of a job is a task or

activity, like tightening a nut. Grouping of tasks, for example, repetitive tightening of nut and placing assembly on tray constitutes a job in motor assembly. Group of jobs forms a department like in above case it would be motor assembly department. Continuing with same example, the motor assembly is the production function of an organisation that finances, markets and produces washing machines. In other words, the start point is task, group of tasks makes a job, group of jobs make a department and group of departments make a function like the production function.

In job design, **method analysis** is used, that is, establishing the proper method for getting the job done. After establishing method and standardising it, **work measurement** is done. Doing work measurement without method study, and then redesigning constitutes wasted effort.

Job Design follows planning and design of product, process and equipment. It involves activities that specify the content of each job and determine how work is distributed within the organisation. It also takes into account the skill set and specialisation of labour.

Method Analysis Aids

Operation chart – A graphic tool to analyse and time elementary motions of Left Hand LH and Right Hand RH (example: Reach, Grasp, Lift, Position, Release) in performing routine, repetitive, short cycle tasks. Theses are also called as therbligs named after Gilbreth who did pioneering micromotion work analysis and build time measuring units TMU for each therblig. This is useful in designing layout of a workplace.

Activity Chart: man machine chart, to identify idle time, analyse and time actions of worker and machine, and assess work load of machine and people.

Flow process charts: to analyse and categorise interstation activities so that the flow of the product throughout the overall production process is represented. This is useful in studies related to design and improvement of plant layout.

Man Machine Activity Chart

<Example: Machining a casting>Not drawn to scale. Can you improve the situation? Time is in mins.

Time(Cum.)	Man		Machine	
1	Unload job		Idle	
3	Clean job		Idle	
4	Clean machine		Idle	
14	Inspect job		Idle	
15	Put aside job		Idle	
16	Pick new job		Idle	
17.8	Load job		Idle	
18	Start machine		Idle	
30	Idle		Machine running	

Working

Idle

% working

M/C 40

Man 60

Total cycle time 30 mins

Job Design

- Operation Chart (Two Hand Operation Chart):Assemble nut and bolt.Can you improve the situation?
- <Existing Situation>

Left Hand		Right Hand	
Reach for nut	⇒	Idle	D
Grasp nut	0	Idle	D
Move towards bolt	⇒	Idle	D
Hold nut	∇	Reach for bolt	⇒
Hold nut	∇	Grasp bolt	0
Hold nut	∇	Move towards nut	⇒
Hold nut	∇	Hold bolt	∇
Assemble nut and bolt	0	Hold assembly	∇
Idle	D	Inspect	□
Idle	D	Release assembly	⇒

Flow Chart

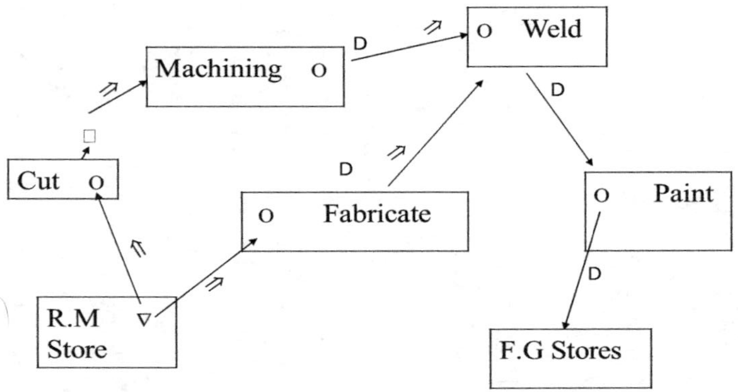
Machining O
O Weld
D
D
Cut O
O Fabricate
D
O Paint
R.M
Store
D
F.G Stores

Symbols used in Charting

° point of origination

O Operation

∇ Storage or Inventory

⇒ Transportation

□ Inspection

D Delay

Delay because of waiting, idling, breakdown and others is Non Value adding and should be eliminated or reduced as a first priority. Next tasks for improvement would be transportation or movement which does not add value unless the business is transportation, and through better layout and material handling methods it can be reduced, if not eliminated. Inventory or Storage is also a waste and should be minimised. Inspection is needed at source and to be done by the person producing or doing the task which implies inspection is built into the process itself. Excessive inspection does not add value.

Last area for improvement would be Operation itself which can be done better through efficient and effective methods, tools and skills, a changed process and increasingly with automation.

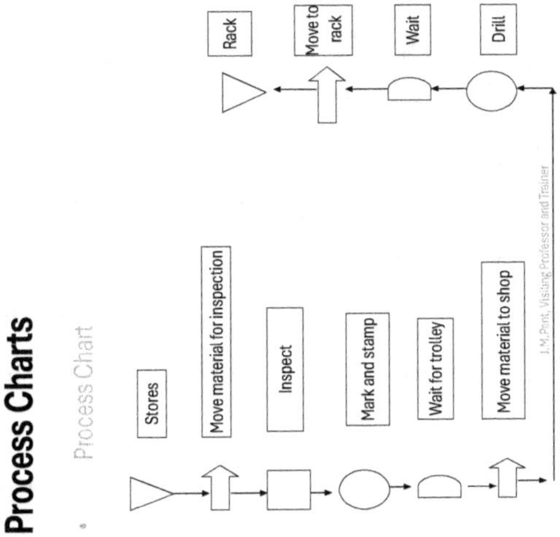
Process Charts
Process Chart
Stores
Move material for inspection
Inspect
Mark and stamp
Wait for trolley
Move material to shop
Drill
Wait
Move to rack
Rack

Principles of Motion Economy

Use the human body the way it works best.

Use natural rhythm of movement.

Symmetrical movement and opposite movement of arms starting and ending at same time.

Neither hand should be idle.

Eye contacts should be few and grouped together.

Minimise number of motions.

Minimise degree of precision and control.

Arrange the workplace to assist performance.

Definite place for all tools and materials.

Tools, materials located close to point of use.

Use mechanical devices to reduce human effort.

Vises and clamps to hold work precisely.

Guides to assist in positioning work without close operator attention.

Controls and foot operated devices can relieve hands of work.

Use gravity.

Work Study: Examination of work systematically investigating factors which affect efficiency in order to effect improvement. It has two main parts:

Method Study

Work Measurement

①Method Study

Systematic recording and critical examination of existing and proposed ways of doing work, for developing and applying easier and more effective methods and reducing costs.

1.Critical Examination (5W1H)

Questioning technique using What, Where, Who, When, Why, and How (5W1H) to understand and improve 'Make Ready', 'Do', and 'Put Away' activities. One should ask a series of primary and secondary questions using 5W1H to understand existing situation, come up with alternatives and finally select one as the improvement..

Purpose:

Existing situation: What is done? Why?

Alternatives What Else?

Improved situation What should?

Principle of improvement-Eliminate unnecessary parts, Minimising, Combine wherever possible

Place

Existing situation: Where is it done? Why?

Alternatives Where Else?

Improved situation Where should it be done?

Principle of improvement: Outsourcing, Location decision, Layout decision

Sequence

Existing situation: When is it done? Why?

Alternatives When Else?

Improved situation When should it be done?

Principle of improvement: Change the order, sequence, Timing, Rearrange.

Person

Existing situation: Who is doing it? Why?

Alternatives Who Else?

Improved situation Who should?

Principle of improvement: Right person for the job, right fit, Retraining, skill improvement, Multiskilling, job enlargement.

Method/Process

Existing situation: How is it done? Why?

Alternatives How Else?

Improved situation How should it be done?

Principle of improvement: Simplify operation, Improve the plan and the method, Minimise non value adding operations.

2. Why Why .. Analysis

Ask why several times to arrive at the root cause of a problem. At least five to six times for most problems. Asking why once only, may lead to a superficial answer, which may not be the real cause. Troubleshooting unreal causes will lead to temporary solutions as the real cause will re-appear after some time.

3. Principle of 5S

Seiri- Sorting. Separating unnecessary from necessary items. Keeping things in order, proper filing etc to reduce search and retrieval time.

Seiton:-Maintain. Keeping the workplace and items well maintained so that they are fit for use when required. Labelling and providing identity.

Seiso-Clean up. Seiso is Inspection. Cleaning the workplace

Seiketsu-Standardisation. Overall Cleanliness.

Shitsuke- Discipline, Habit. Have a positive and disciplined work attitude.

4.Lateral thinking

Allows you to try different perceptions and different points. It allows you to do out of the box thinking, removing the mental road blocks to creativity. Logic is concerned with 'the truth', with what is, but lateral thinking is concerned with possibilities, with what might be.

② Work Measurement

Work Measurement is the application of techniques designed to establish time for a qualified worker to carry out a specified job at a designed level of performance. The techniques used are Time Study, Work Sampling, Synthesis from standard data and Pre-determined motion time systems

Time Study

1.Selecting job: new job, change of material or method, planning incentive scheme, plant utilisation/ bottleneck operation study, excessive cost of job..

2.Qualified representative worker: has physical attributes, intelligence, education, skill and knowledge to carry work to satisfactory standards of safety, quality, and quantity.

3.Obtaining, recording all information about job, operator, and surrounding conditions.

4.Time Study: involves checking method of doing work, breaking job into elements, timing and rating of person doing the job.Time study requires a study board, time study sheet and time measuring device. Time can be measured using Stop Watch method and Video Camera method. Stop watch method can use snap back method and continuous time method

5.From Time Study to Standard Time

Observed Time OT

Normal Time (NT) = OT X Rating

Standard Time = NT/(1-A) where A is the Allowance fraction

Allowances: are for personal needs, basic fatigue and in addition there are variable allowances depending on nature of work like standing, abnormal position, overhead, weight handled, light, heat and air conditions, visual, mental and aural strain, monotony mental and physical, start up, shut down, set up, tool change, and so forth.

Work Sampling

Work Sampling is a technique in which a large number of instantaneous observations are made over a period of time of a group of machines, processes or workers to statistically estimate the percentage working and idle time of people and equipment. Then on basis of

	No. of observations	Total	%
Machine Running	||||	5	62
Machine stopped	|||	3	38

number of units produced in that time period, the standard time per unit can be estimated..

<Example>

$$S^*p = 2 * \sqrt{(p(1-p)/N)}$$

where S is the accuracy, N is the number of observations, p is the percentage working or idle time, and confidence level is 95.4%. This formula works out the number of observations needed to make a fair estimate of p.

Predetermine Motion Time Systems (PMTS). This is used to build up standard time for manual work, based on time standards available for basic human motions.

One of the techniques under PMTS is Method Time Measurement (MTM). MTM analyses basic human motions and measures time in TMU (Time measurement unit: 1 TMU = 0.0006 mins or 0.00001 hrs)

Synthesis from Time Standards

This method involves breaking down the work into its basic elements, each with an established time standard derived from historical data, time studies, or predetermined motion time systems. By summing these elemental times, managers can accurately estimate the total time necessary for a job.

Job Design

- Procedure of Work Study

	Basic Step	Method Study	Work Measurement
1	Select jobs for study	✓	✓
2	**Record**	✓	✓
	Various charts, Diagrams, Movement analysis		
3	Examine (critical examination, 5W1H)	✓	
4	Develop	✓	
5	Measure(stop watch, PMTS, Work sampling, etc.)		✓
6	Define	✓	✓
7	Instal	✓	✓
8	Maintain	✓	✓
9	**Charts**: Operation Process Chart/Outline process chart Flow Process chart Two Handed process charts	✓	
	Multple Activity Chart	✓	
	Travel chart, flow Diagram, String Diagram	✓	

Value Engineering VE

Value engineering is a proven management technique using a systematised approach to seek out the best functional balance between the cost, reliability and performance of a product, service or project. Developed by Lawrence D Miles, U.S.A.

VE is: Systems oriented, Multidisciplinary, Function oriented and Life cycle oriented. It saves money, provides better value leading to customer delight. VE is not intended to correct omissions made in design nor review calculations made by designer. VE is not quality control. VE does not cut cost sacrificing quality, function, reliability and performance.

Value Programs

Value Engineering: Describes a value study on a project, product or service that is being developed, modified, re-designed.

Value Analysis: Describes a value study of a project or product, service that is already built or designed and analyses the product to see if it can be improved.

Value Management: Identifies the methodology and techniques used in value work, but does not distinguish between engineering of a building or facility and the analysis of a product. It is used to describe the entire field of value endeavours.

What is Value?

Aristotle thought of Value like political value, ethical value, social value, religious value, economic value, aesthetic value, judicial value. ***VE is concerned with Economic Value*** namely **cost value**, **use value**, **esteem** or aesthetic value, exchange or **market value**.

Value has relationship with both cost and the required function of the product, service or system.

Value = Function/Cost

Value can be increased by:

1.Enhancing function at same cost

2.Same function is provided at reduced cost

3.Improvement in function and reduction in cost

4.Improvement in function but corresponding less increase in cost

Function

Function is the purpose of an object-product, service, process or system. If the functions are achieved as desired by customer, the object is of value or use.

Two types of functions:

1.Use function

2.Sell function

Levels of function: Basic or primary function, and Secondary function

Defining a Function

Function –Defining A Function

- Function to be defined in two words-an active VERB and a measurable NOUN.
- <Example> Screwdriver
- What does a screwdriver do?

Deliver torque	Transmit torque	Withstand torque	Receive torque

- The basic function is deliver torque. If this is eliminated, the screwdriver does not exist.
- All other functions are secondary functions.

Jems Consultancy Services

Function-Verb And Noun -Examples

Use functions

Verbs	Verbs	Verbs	Verbs
Absorb	Convey	Insulate	Store
Apply	Filter	Protect	Lift
Control	Generate	Support	Emit
Noun	**Noun**	**Noun**	**Noun**
Corrosion	Flow	Waste	Weight
Current	Friction	Power	Warpage
Contamination	Material	Torque	Transport

Sell functions

Verbs	Noun	Noun	Noun
Improve	Appearance	Effect	Style
Increase	Convenience	Features	Comfort
Add	Colours	Flavours	SKUs

Jems Consultancy Services

Cost

Cost

- Customers want Value for Money.
- This Value depends on Cost of product
- Price=Cost + Profit
- VE deals with Cost only.
- Elements of Cost
  - Direct Material
  - Direct Labour
  - Direct expenses
  - Overheads-Production, Adminstration, Marketing, Sales, Distribution, and Financial
- Product, service, process or system cost have to be transferred to Function cost.

Jems Consultancy Services

Worth

Worth is the minimum cost of achieving a Function (basic and secondary) without tradeoff on performance. Evaluation of Worth is comparison with some other items which fulfills the same function.

Value Gap=Existing Cost – Worth

Value Index = Existing Cost/Worth

Value is always relative and established with reference to a value standard, which we are calling as Worth which is the dollar equivalent of the performance of a product. It is subjective.

Phases of VE project and study

1.Orientation phase-project selection, team members

2.Information phase

3.Function phase

4.Creative phase

5.Evaluation phase

6.Recommendation phase

7.mplementation phase

8.Audit phase

1.Project Selection Process

- VE Project can be selected by the VE group(indicative list below)
  Or VE Project can be given by management
- Tools-market survey, focus groups, VOC, customer complaints, warranty claims, quality and engineering reports, Pareto chart

VE Project can be selected based on design factor such as:	***VE Project can be selected based on these factors/ problems***:
Tight tolerance specifications	High rejections, scrap
Use of non standard items	Low material yield
Use of special types of materials	High warranty claims
Too many components in assembly	Poor customer satisfaction, customer complaints, returns
Heavy weight	High rework
VE Project based on Time factor:	High throughput time
Design developed long time back	Inventories increase
Design development, Procurement, Processing time	High wastages-time,material,m/c

Jems Consultancy Services

Pareto Principle

- VE calls for identifying unnecessary costs.
- To identify a potential VE project which can provide higher ROI, Pareto principle of separating the ***vital few (20% making up 80% of problems/impact)*** from the ***trivial many (rest 80%)*** can be used.

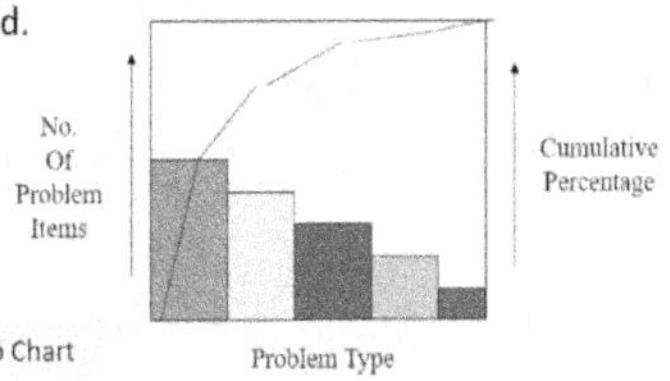
No. Of Problem Items
Cumulative Percentage
Problem Type

Pareto Chart

Jems Consultancy Services

VE Team

Multidisciplinary team approach-for example, depending on the problem and nature of project, team members may be selected from: Design, Architecture,Projects, Planning, Engineering, Tool room, tooling, mould, jigs, fixtures, Maintenance, Utilities, Manufacturing/Production, Process, Quality, Finance, Costing, Purchase, Stores, Material Planning, Supply chain, Logistics,Marketing, Sales, Customer relationship management.

Team should have regular meeting once a week

Team members should have sense of ownership.

2.Information Phase

Project Goals: Project Mission Statement to be stated in clear and precise terms as to what this project will accomplish for the organisation or its customers; define the problem statement; describe the "burning platform" for this project. Why is this project necessary?

Should be **SMART** goals-specific, Measurable and verifiable, attainable, real and time bound.

Project Scope: define the boundaries for this project. What will be addressed? What will not be addressed?

Scope creepL As activities are developed, be certain that they do not go beyond the project's original scope.

Scope drift: Project focus gradually moves away from its original charter.

Cost: Collect all cost and estimate cost where not available.

Facts : Study, analysis and improvement should be based on facts though observation and data.

2.Information Phase

Information gathering-indicative questions for making a check list to understand existing situation

• Part no., Part description • Manufactured or bought out • Standard or non standard • Design specifications and tolerances • Materials specification • Process of manufacture • Are specific materials easily available? • Who is the user?	Does it have manufacturing problems? Does it have customer complaint, returns, warranty claims problem? Is there change in original design? Why? Who is in charge of manufacturing, design, quality, purchase, sales, others

Jems Consultancy Services

3.Function Analyse Phase

This is at the heart of VE concept.

Four basic questions

1.What does it do?

2.What must it do?

3.What does it cost now?

4.What must it cost?

The tools to be used in this phase are:

1.Function-Cost-Worth Analysis

2.Function Analysis System Technique (FAST

Determine functions

1.The product/ service/system should be divided into components/ activities/ procedures.

2.The functions of each component/activity/ procedure should be defined in two words- active **Verb** and measurable **Noun**.

3.The cost of each component/ activity/ procedure has to be ascertained. If there is a price, reduce it to cost taking a reasonable percentage of profit.

4.The cost of each component/ activity/ procedure has to be transformed into functions, based on technical considerations.

5.Value - Total of cost of functions=cost of component/activity/ procedure.

Function Analyse Phase

Function Analysis				
Component	Function		Type	Remark
	Verb	Noun		

Transformation to Function Cost					
Component	Existing cost (Rs)	Function		Type	Existing Function Cost (Rs)
		Verb	Noun		
A					
B					

Jems Consultancy Services

Function Analyse Phase

Function-Cost-Worth Matrix							
Component	Function		Existing cost (Rs)	Worth	Method of Achieving worth	Value Gap/Value Index	Rank
	Verb	Noun					
A							
B							
C							

Jems Consultancy Services

Function Analyse Phase

- **Create a function logic diagram (FAST-Function Analysis System Technique)**

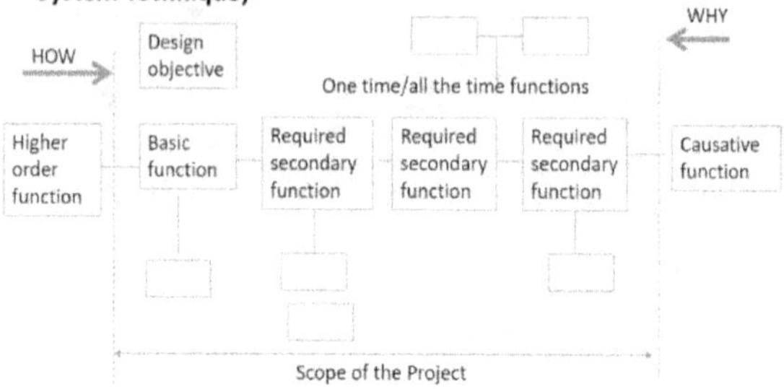

WHY
HOW
Design objective
One time/all the time functions
Higher order function
Basic function
Required secondary function
Required secondary function
Required secondary function
Causative function
Scope of the Project

Jems Consultancy Services

Function Analyse Phase

- **Drawing FAST diagram-** Example screwdriver
- Components of screw driver
- Blade
- Shank
- Handle

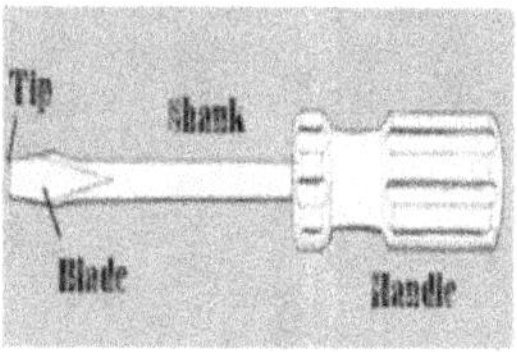

Tip
Shank
Blade
Handle

Jems Consultancy Services

Function Analyse Phase

HOW	Drive Screw	Deliver Torque	WHY

The higher order function is a requirement of the component under study and that is 'Drive Screw'.

Function Analysis Matrix		
Component	Functions	
	Verb	Noun
Blade	Suit	Slot
Shank	Transmit	Torque
Handle	Facilitate	Grip

Function Analyse Phase

- **FAST-<Example Screwdriver>**

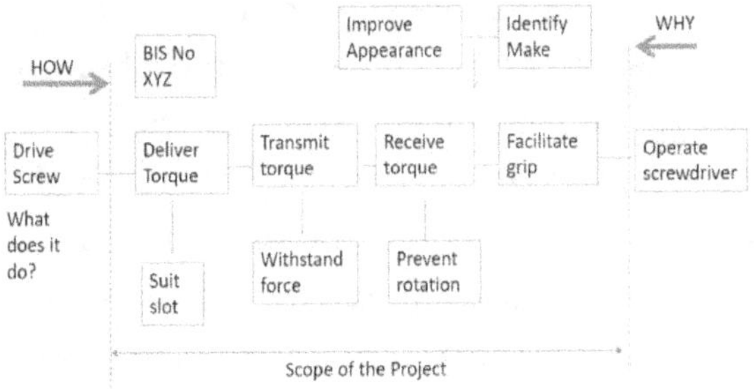
HOW
WHY
BIS No XYZ
Improve Appearance
Identify Make
Drive Screw
Deliver Torque
Transmit torque
Receive torque
Facilitate grip
Operate screwdriver
What does it do?
Suit slot
Withstand force
Prevent rotation
Scope of the Project

4.Creative Phase

Creative thought process is composed of three main categories:① Imagination, ② Inspiration, ③ Illumination. Einstein once said that "imagination is more important than knowledge" Enthusiasm drives imagination to endless limits. Inspiration is the trigger (stimuli) for developing something new using knowledge and experience of the team. Illumination is when the idea rises from sub conscious to conscious mind.

The central theme of the creative phase is "what else could do the same needed functions?"

Few ways of generating creative ideas are brainstorming, attribute listing like colour, size, weight etc. and combining, morphological analysis by breakdown and association, lateral thinking, why..why analysis. Check list method is developing a new idea through a list of related issues like can we put it to other uses? Modify? Magnify? Minify? Substitute? Rearrange? Reverse? Combine? Simplify? Eliminate?

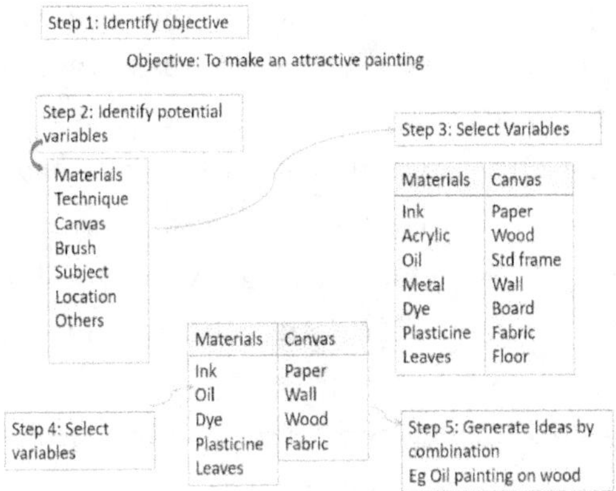
Step 1: Identify objective
Objective: To make an attractive painting
Step 2: Identify potential variables
Materials
Technique
Canvas
Brush
Subject
Location
Others
Step 3: Select Variables
Materials
Canvas
Ink
Acrylic
Oil
Metal
Dye
Plasticine
Leaves
Paper
Wood
Std frame
Wall
Board
Fabric
Floor
Materials
Canvas
Ink
Oil
Dye
Plasticine
Leaves
Paper
Wall
Wood
Fabric
Step 4: Select variables
Step 5: Generate Ideas by combination
Eg Oil painting on wood

Combination of Variables to Generate Ideas

Power supply	Bulb type	Size	Style	Finish	Material
Battery	LED	Very large	Modern	Black	Metal
Mains	Sodium vapour	Large	Antique	White	Ceramic
Solar	Incandescent	Medium	Ethnic	Metallic	Glass
Crank	Daylight	Small	Industrial	Natural	Wood
Generator	Coloured	Hand held	Roman	Fabric	Plastic

Ideas for lighting manufacturer

5.Evaluation Phase

This phase aims at finding out the best alternative. ***The evaluation process involves***: ①Finding out the parameters for evaluation, ②Fixing the weightage for parameters ③Evaluate alternatives for decision making- eliminate ideas which will not work,combine ideas, categorise and rank them, and cost benefit analysis

Tools to be used are: Brainstorming, Evaluation matrix, Life cycle costing.

Evaluation Matrix

	Parameters	Weightage
1	Fuel consumption	35
2	Reliability	30
3	Maintenance cost	20
4	Riding comfort	10
5	Appearance	5
	Total	100

Weighted Evaluation method
Example: Weightages for purchase of motorcycle
Weights could be equal or unequal)

Forced Decision Matrix
Two parameters compared at a time, 1 for what is more important, 0 for the other

	1	2	3	4	5	6	7	8	9	10	Total	%
1	0	1	1	1							3	30
2	1				1	1	1				4	40
3		0			0			1	1		2	20
4			0			0		0		1	1	10
5				0			0		0	0	0	0

Jems Consultancy Services

6.Development Phase

Refine and develop ideas, Improve, Simplify, Combine, Reverse, Eliminate, do Concurrently, Reduce number of parts, fasteners, joints, and so forth.

Overcome obstacles as people resist Change and remove negativity.

7.Presentation Phase

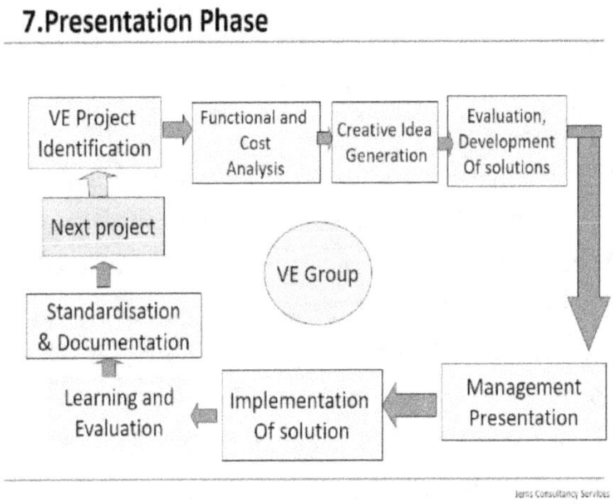
7.Presentation Phase
VE Project Identification
Functional and Cost Analysis
Creative Idea Generation
Evaluation, Development Of solutions
Next project
VE Group
Standardisation & Documentation
Learning and Evaluation
Implementation Of solution
Management Presentation

8.Implementation Phase

8.Implementation Phase

- VE team has to formulate an implementation plan.
- ***Plan, Do, Check and Act***
- The plan must be executed, then reviewed and action taken to bridge the gap between actual and plan, and to improve the plan.
- Audit: ① Operational audit② Financial audit

Implementation Plan

Sl. No	Action point	What is to be done	How	Who will do	Where	Start time	Completion time

[illegible] Consultancy Services

Practice

Information phase: What is being done now? Who is doing it? What could it do? What must it not do?

Measure: How will the alternatives be measured?

Analyse :What are the alternate ways of meeting requirements? What else can perform the desired function? What must be done? What does it cost?

Generate: What else will do the job?

Evaluate: Which Ideas are the best?

Develop and expand ideas: What are the impacts? What is the cost? What is the performance?

Present ideas

Sell alternatives

23
Maintenance Management and TPM

Maintenance management involves the processes and activities required to keep equipment, machinery, and infrastructure in optimal working condition.. Effective maintenance ensures operational efficiency, minimises downtime, increases equipment availability, extends equipment lifespan, and enhances safety.

Types of Maintenance

Preventive Maintenance: Scheduled, and routine maintenance to prevent equipment failures.

Predictive Maintenance: Monitoring and analysing data to predict and address potential issues before they cause failures.

Corrective Maintenance: Repairing or replacing equipment after a failure has occurred.

Condition-Based Maintenance performed based on the actual condition of equipment, often using sensors and real-time data.

Maintenance Strategies

Time-Based Maintenance: Regular maintenance at fixed intervals regardless of equipment condition.

Usage-Based Maintenance: Maintenance based on the equipment's operational usage (e.g., hours run, cycles completed).

Reliability-Centered Maintenance (RCM): A structured approach focusing on identifying and maintaining critical equipment functions.

Total Productive Maintenance (TPM): Involving all employees in proactive maintenance to improve overall equipment effectiveness (OEE).

Maintenance Planning and Scheduling

Planning : Determining what maintenance tasks are needed and allocating resources for those tasks.

Scheduling : Timing maintenance activities to minimize disruption and ensure that resources are available.

Maintenance Performance Metrics

Mean Time Between Failures (MTBF): The average time between equipment breakdowns.

MTBF = Total Operating Time/ Number of Failures

Mean Time to Repair (MTTR): The average time required to repair equipment and restore it to operational status.
MTTR = Total Repair Time/ Number of Repairs

Overall Equipment Effectiveness (OEE): A measure of how well equipment is performing relative to its full potential.
OEE = Availability X Performance Rate X Quality Rate

Availability = Operating(or Running) Time/ Total Available(or Loading)Time
Available(or Loading)Time =Total Time(in shift, or day) – Planned Stoppage time
Operating (or Running) Time = Available (or Loading Time) – Downtime (Failures, set ups)
Performance Rate = Actual Output/ Target or Standard Output
Actual output may be less than standard output because of minor stoppages and reduced speed.
Quality Rate = Good output/ Actual Output

Good output is less than actual output because of scrap, rejections, defectives.

Availability (Operating Rate) can be improved by eliminating breakdowns, reducing set-ups and adjustment losses, and other stoppages
Performance Rate can be improved by eliminating speed losses, minor stoppages, and idling.
Quality (Rate Of Quality Products) can be improved by eliminating quality defects in the process and during start-up.

Tools and Technologies in Maintenance Management

Computerized Maintenance Management Systems (CMMS): Software that helps manage maintenance activities, track work orders, and store maintenance data.
Internet of Things (IoT): Connected devices and sensors providing real-time data for predictive and condition-based maintenance.
Drones and Robotics: Used for inspection and maintenance in hard-to-reach areas.

TPM

TPM is a comprehensive approach to maintenance that involves all employees, from top management to the shop floor, to proactively maintain equipment and improve overall operational efficiency.

8 Pillars of TPM:

1. ***Autonomous Maintenance:*** Operators are trained to perform basic maintenance tasks such as cleaning, lubricating, and inspecting equipment, thus fostering ownership and early problem detection.

2. ***Planned Maintenance***: A scheduled approach that aims to achieve zero breakdowns through systematic maintenance activities.

3. ***Quality Maintenance***: Ensuring equipment consistently produces high-quality products by addressing root causes of defects and variances.

4. ***Focused Improvement (Kaizen)***: Continuous improvement initiatives that aim to enhance equipment performance through small, incremental changes.

5. ***Early Equipment Management***: Integrating maintenance considerations into the design and commissioning of new

equipment to enhance reliability and maintainability.

6. ***Training and Education***: Developing a skilled workforce capable of performing maintenance tasks and understanding equipment operation.

7. ***Safety, Health, and Environment***: Ensuring maintenance activities do not compromise safety and environmental standards.

8. ***Office TPM***: Extending TPM principles to administrative functions to improve overall efficiency.

Please also see slides which follow.

Preventive Medicine for Equipment = Preventive Maintenance

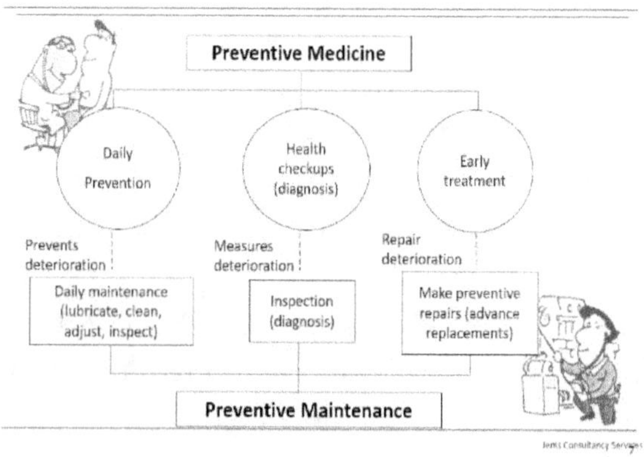

Preventive Medicine
Daily Prevention
Health checkups (diagnosis)
Early treatment
Prevents deterioration
Measures deterioration
Repair deterioration
Daily maintenance (lubricate, clean, adjust, inspect)
Inspection (diagnosis)
Make preventive repairs (advance replacements)
Preventive Maintenance

Progress of Maintenance Activity

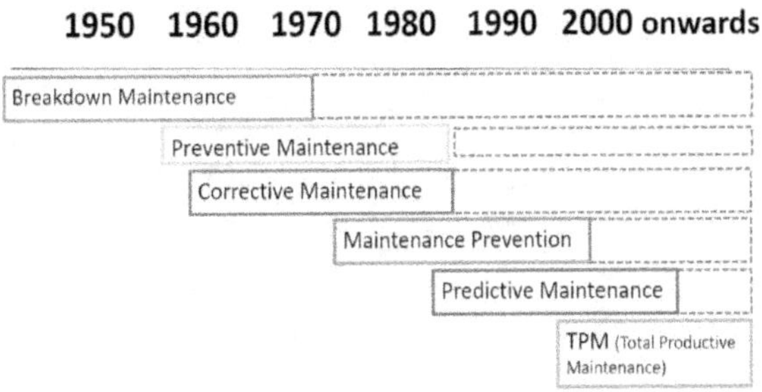
1950 1960 1970 1980 1990 2000 onwards
Breakdown Maintenance
Preventive Maintenance
Corrective Maintenance
Maintenance Prevention
Predictive Maintenance
TPM (Total Productive Maintenance)

Jems Consultancy Services

"My job is to pick up these bottles!"
"My job is stop these bottles from falling down"

BEFORE TPM **AFTER TPM**

Jems Consultancy Services

Major Losses Considered In TPM

LOSS CATEGORIES	THE SEVEN BIG LOSSES
Downtime (Lost availability)	▪ Breakdowns-Equipment failures ▪Adjustments ▪Tool, die changeover/set ups
Speed losses (Lost performance)	▪ Idling and minor stoppages ▪ Reduced speed operations
Defect losses (Lost quality)	▪ Quality loss- Scrap and rework ▪ Startup losses

Unforeseen And Chronic Losses

- Unforeseen (sporadic) losses- sudden breakdowns and defects
  - Comparatively easy to get at the causes of breakdowns
  - Easy to work out countermeasures because of clear cause and effect relationship.
- Chronic losses
  - Cause is not clearly known
  - New countermeasures needed

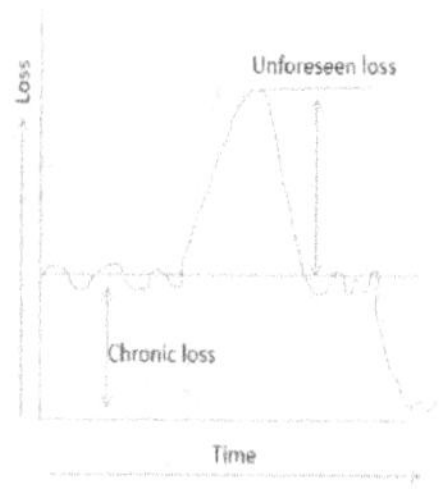
Loss
Unforeseen loss
Chronic loss
Time

Stages Leading To Breakdown

1. Stage One: Potential Minor Defects
2. Stage Two: Visible Minor Defects
3. Stage Three: Reduced Minor Efficiency
3. Stage Four: Short Stoppages
3. Stage Five: Breakdown

Jems Consultancy Services

Five Countermeasures To Reduce Breakdowns

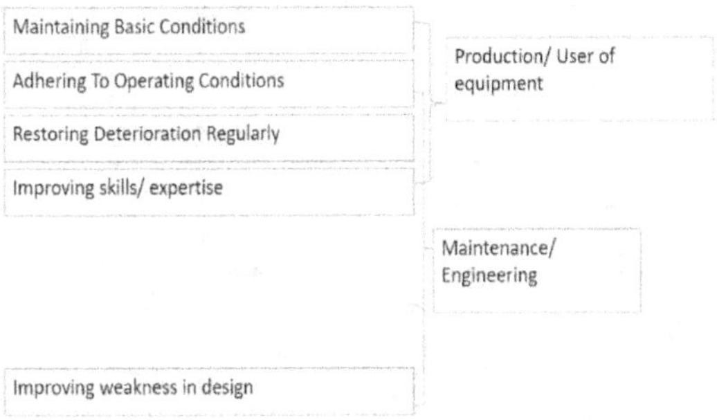

Maintaining Basic Conditions
Adhering To Operating Conditions
Restoring Deterioration Regularly
Improving skills/ expertise
Production/ User of equipment
Maintenance/ Engineering
Improving weakness in design

Jems Consultancy Services

Abnormality

Fugai

TPM
Abnormality detected

Equipment--------------------------------
Work area --------------------------------
Date of detection-------------------------
Person who detected------------------
Abnormality details

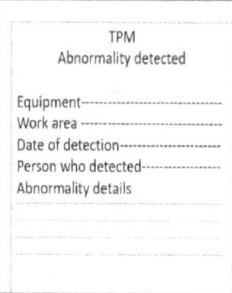

White tag-faults that can be corrected by operators themselves.

Red tag-faults that need to be corrected by Maintenance.

Tag to be tied to machine and one copy for record.

Diagram Of Overall Equipment Effectiveness (OEE)

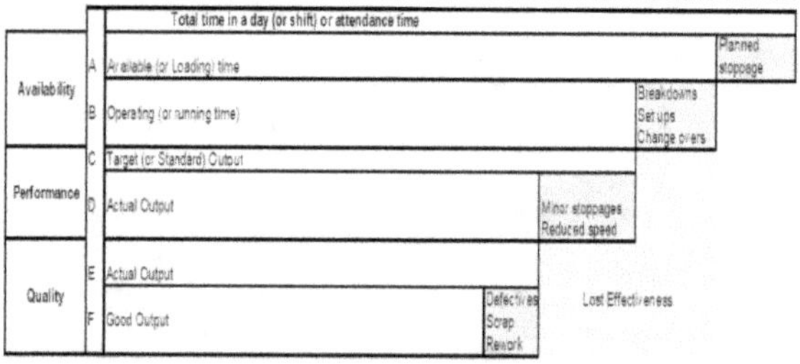
Total time in a day (or shift) or attendance time
Availability
A Available (or Loading) time
Planned stoppage
B Operating (or running time)
Breakdowns
Set ups
Change overs
Performance
C Target (or Standard) Output
D Actual Output
Minor stoppages
Reduced speed
Quality
E Actual Output
F Good Output
Defectives
Scrap
Rework
Lost Effectiveness

OEE (Overall Equipment Effectiveness) = (B/A) * (D/C) * (F/E)
= Availability rate X Performance rate X Quality rate

24
Kaizen

Kaizen is incremental and continual improvement through elimination of waste. It is a Japanese way of improvement and evolving a quality culture involving all people. It is a combination of Kai meaning to modify and change, and Zen meaning to think, to make good and better.

Wherever there is a method or process, there is an opportunity for doing it in a better way.

Any work which does not add Value, that takes one away from one's goal, is a Waste. It could be excess movement, transportation, inventory, defects-scrap, rejects, customer returns, rework, waiting-delays, idling, stoppages, extra processing, bad system or method, low speed, lack of plan, unutilised people's creativity, line imbalance, strain, large variation, uneven output, excess paperwork, system downtime etc.

The heart of Kaizen is rotating the PDCA cycle and standardising after every stage of improvement, then improving the plan and repeating PDCA. Continuously doing PDCA brings progress.

Plan (P)-formulate and define the problem and think countermeasures using various problem-solving tools. Do (D)-execute the plan. Check (C) – whether things happened as per plan. Action (A) – modify or improve the plan.

Kaizen is the umbrella for all improvement processes and tools covered in this book.

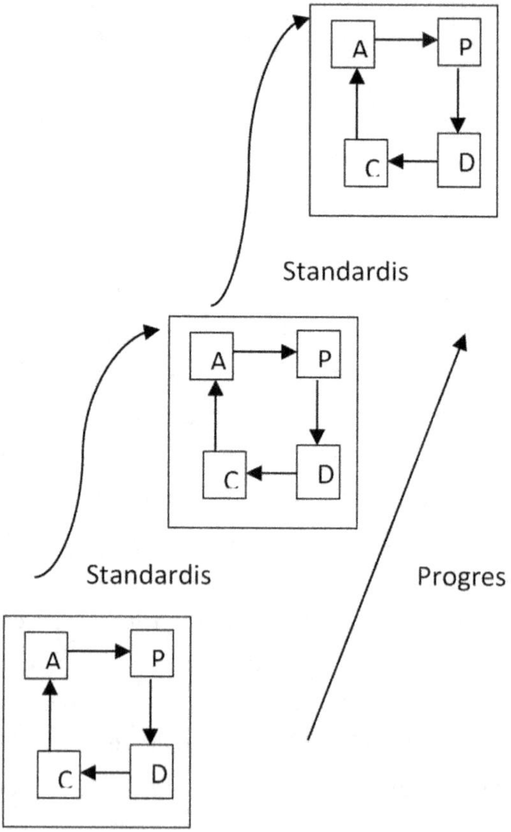

A
P
C
D
Standardis
A
P
C
D
Standardis
Progres
A
P
C
D

If plan is successful, standardise it and go for an improved plan, and continue with iterations and increase in challenging goals.

PDCA and Problem Solving

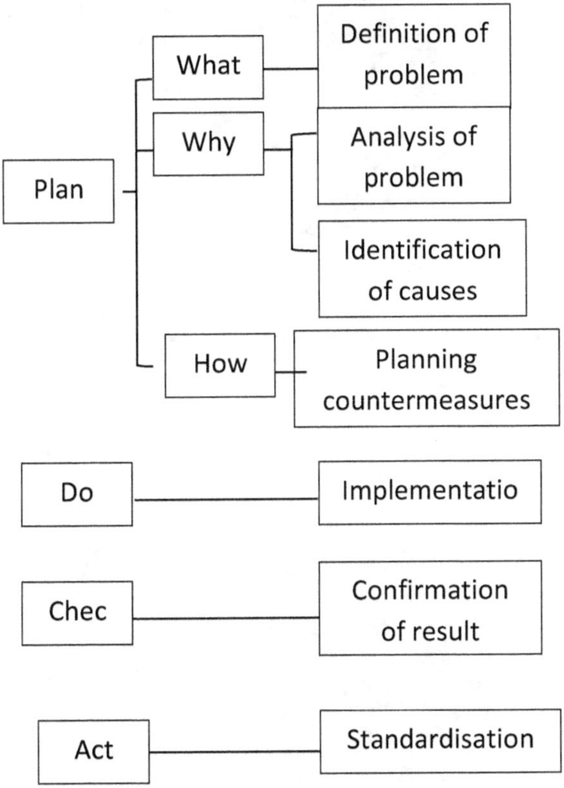

Plan
What
Definition of problem
Why
Analysis of problem
Identification of causes
How
Planning countermeasures
Do
Implementatio
Chec
Confirmation of result
Act
Standardisation

Waste is Money: A Rupee Saved is a Rupee Earned

Kaizen is continuous elimination of waste

J.M.Pant, Management Consultant, Trainer and Visiting Professor
Cell (0)9811030273, e-mail jm.pant@gmail.com

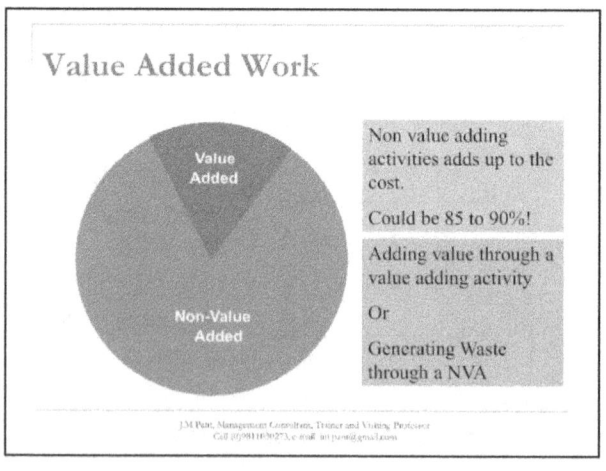

Value Added Work

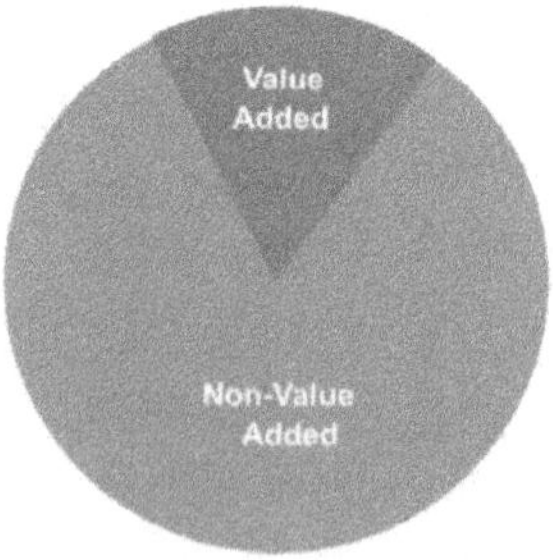
Value Added
Non-Value Added

Non value adding activities adds up to the cost.

Could be 85 to 90%!

Adding value through a value adding activity

Or

Generating Waste through a NVA

J.M.Pant, Management Consultant, Trainer and Visiting Professor
Cell (0)9811030273, e-mail jm.pant@gmail.com

25
Lean Management and the Toyota Production System

Lean Management is a systematic approach to streamlining processes and eliminating waste to create more value for customers. Originating in the manufacturing sector, Lean principles have since been adopted across various industries, including services, healthcare, and software development. The core idea is to maximize efficiency by identifying and removing activities that do not add value.

The Principles of Lean Management

1. ***Value***: is what meets the customer needs and satisfaction; what does not is Waste or Non Value Adding.
2. ***Value Stream***: is mapping out the entire value flow for each product or service, identifying all steps in the process and distinguishing between value-adding and non-value-adding activities.

3. ***Flow*** ensures that the value-adding steps occur in a tight sequence so that the product or service moves smoothly towards the customer.
4. ***Pull***: system where production is based on actual customer demand rather than forecasted demand, reducing overproduction and excess inventory.
5. ***Kaizen*** or continuous improvement by constantly seeking ways to enhance processes and eliminate waste.

The Toyota Production System (TPS)

The Toyota Production System (TPS) is the original framework from which Lean Management principles were derived. Developed by Toyota in the mid-20th century, TPS focuses on improving efficiency and quality through the elimination of waste and continuous improvement, provides flexibility, employee engagement and sustainable environmentally friendly operations.

Key Elements of TPS

1. **Just-In-Time (JIT)**

<Example>: Toyota's assembly lines receive parts from suppliers precisely when needed for

production, reducing the need for large inventories and storage space.

2. ***Kaizen***:

<Example>: Toyota employees regularly participate in Kaizen events, where they collaborate to identify waste and develop solutions to improve them.

3. ***Kanban***:.

<Example>: In a Toyota plant, Kanban cards signal the need for more parts on the assembly line, ensuring a smooth flow without overproduction and minimising inventory.

4. ***Heijunka***: or production levelling, is the practice of smoothing out production schedules to avoid excessive batching and reduce variability. This helps in balancing workload and minimizing waste.

<Example>: Toyota levels production schedules to ensure a consistent and predictable flow of products, avoiding peaks and troughs in manufacturing.

5. ***Jidoka*** is automation with a human touch, and emphasises the importance of quality and stopping production to fix problems as they occur. This prevents defects from passing through the production line.

<Example>: Toyota assembly lines are equipped with Andon cords that workers can pull to stop production if they detect a problem, allowing immediate resolution and preventing defective products from moving forward.

A story of the power of Kaizen at Toyota

At Toyota, the principle of Kaizen has led to countless small but impactful changes over the years. One famous example involves a suggestion from a line worker who noticed that adjusting the angle of a parts bin by a few degrees made it easier and faster to retrieve parts. This minor adjustment, replicated across the production line, resulted in significant time savings and efficiency improvements. Such stories highlight how small, continuous improvements can collectively lead to substantial operational enhancements.

26

Quality Management and Six Sigma

Listen to the President of a typical manufacturing company:

'Our scrap and rework costs this year were five times our profit. Because of those costs, we have to increase our selling price and we subsequently lost market share. Quality is no longer a technical issue; it is a business issue.'

Quality management is a crucial aspect of Operations that focuses on ensuring products and services meet or exceed customer expectations. The product design and quality specifications evolve as per the customer requirement and the approach is known as Quality Function Deployment (QFD).

Our forefathers knew,-as we know,-that quality is important. Metrology, specifications, inspection- all go back many centuries before the Christian era. Following World War II, two major forces emerged that have had a profound impact on quality.

The **first** was the Japanese revolution in quality. Prior to World War II, many Japanese products were perceived , throughout the world, to be poor in quality. To help sell their products in international markets, the Japanese took some revolutionary steps to improve quality: The senior managers personally took charge of leading the revolution. All levels and functions received training in the quality disciplines. Quality improvement projects were undertaken on a continuing basis-at a revolutionary pace.

The **second** major force was the prominence of product quality in the public mind. Quality has become a cardinal priority for most organizations because of competition, changing customer attitude towards quality and higher quality expectations, changing product mix and product complexity.

Quality Management involves a range of practices including quality planning, inspection, quality control and quality improvement. It has historically moved from Inspection alone and inspection oriented Quality Control (Prior 1945) to Statistical

Quality Control SQC (1945-55) which is now Statistical Process Control SPC, and Quality Assurance (1955-70), Total Quality Management TQM and Six Sigma.

Quality Gurus

Dr Shewart spent his professional career at Western Electric and Bell Telephone Laboratories, both divisions of AT&T. He developed control chart theory with control limits, and tracking, analysing and taking actions based on assignable and chance causes of variation. He also developed the PDSA (Plan> Do>Study>Act) cycle for learning and improvement.

Dr W.Edwards Deming was the protégé of Shewart. In 1950, he taught statistical process control and the importance of quality to the leading CEOs of Japanese industry. He is credited with creating the foundation for the Japanese quality miracle, and resurgence as an economic power.

Deming's 14 points provide a theory for management to improve quality, productivity and competitive position.

Deming's 14 points:

1. Create and publish the aims and purpose of the organization.
2. Learn the new philosophy
3. Understand the purpose of inspection
4. Stop awarding business based on price alone.
5. Improve constantly and forever the system.
6. Institute training
7. Teach and institute leadership
8. Drive out fear, create trust, and create a climate for innovation.
9. Optimise the efforts of teams, groups, and staff areas.
10. Eliminate exhortations for the work force.
11. Eliminate numerical quotas for the work force.
12. Eliminate management by objective
13. Remove barriers that rob people of pride and workmanship
14. Encourage education and self improvement for all.

Dr Juran contemporary to Dr Deming is famous for Juran's trilogy for managing quality through interrelated processes of ***planning, control and improvement***

Dr Philip Crossby

1.Defined quality as a conformity to certain specifications set forth by management and not some vague concept of "goodness."

"Do It Right the First Time" as this is less expensive.

2.Focused on zero defects as the performance standard.

3.Prevention of non-conformance is the objective, not appraisal.

4."Quality is Free."

Non conformity is costly while good quality is free.

Dr Taguchi

Dr Taguchi developed the Quality Loss Function which combines cost, target and variation into one metric. Emphasis is on robustness of design parameters and tolerances.

Dr Ishikawa

Dr Ishikawa studied under Deming and Juran, and adapted the total quality control concept for the Japanese. He is best known for fish bone diagram (also Ishikawa diagram or cause and effect diagram). He developed the quality circle concept in Japan which are small work groups trained in SPC concepts which meet regularly to identify and solve quality problems in their work environment

Principles of Quality Management

Customer Focus: Understanding and meeting customer needs and expectations is paramount.
Leadership: Leaders must establish a clear vision and direction for quality improvement.
Engagement of People: Employees at all levels must be engaged and empowered to contribute to quality goals.
Process Approach: Managing activities as processes ensures consistency and efficiency.
Continuous Improvement: Ongoing efforts to improve products, services, and processes.
Measurement, Evidence-Based Decision Making: Decisions should be based on data analysis and evaluation. What cannot be measured cannot be controlled.
Relationship Management Building strong relationships with suppliers and stakeholders.

Quality Management System (QMS) provides a framework for consistent quality control and improvement. ISO 9001:2015 is a widely recognized standard for QMS that outlines requirements for a systematic approach to managing quality. Implementing a QMS involves establishing quality policies and objectives, documenting processes and procedures, and regularly reviewing and improving the system using QC tools, brainstorming. problem solving techniques and creativity.

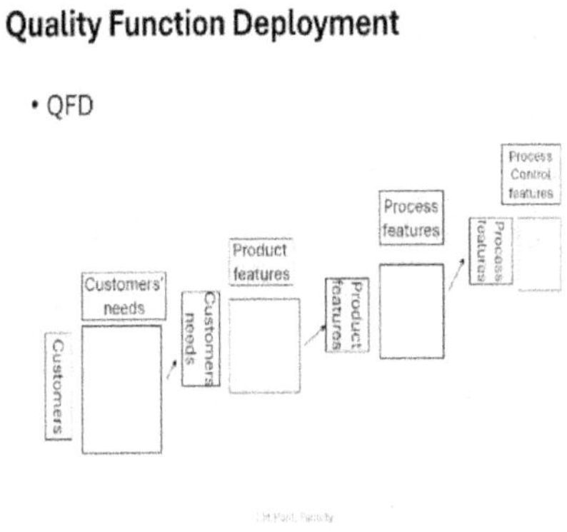
Quality Function Deployment
• QFD
Customers
Customers' needs
Customers needs
Product features
Product features
Process features
Process features
Process Control features

QFD-Mapping customer requirement to product and process specifications.

Quality Function Deployment

- House of Quality (Example)

Correlations entered
In squares like:
Strong positive, positive,
Negative,
Strong negative

Technical requirements →		Paper width	Paper thickness	Coating thickness	Tensile strength	Paper color	Competitive evaluation
Importance to customer / Customer requirements ↓							X = Us A = Competitor A B = Competitor B (5 is best) 1 2 3 4 5
Paper will not tear	3	◇	○		⊙		X A B
Consistent finish	1			○			A X B
No ink bleed	2		⊙	○			B A X
Prints clearly	3			⊙		○	X A B

Relationships
⊙Strong=9
○ Medium = 3
◇ Small=1

J.M.Parl, Faculty

Tools and techniques used

Statistical Process Control (SPC): Uses statistical methods to monitor and control processes.

Six Sigma: A data-driven approach aimed at reducing defects and variability. *Lean Management*: Focuses on eliminating waste and optimizing processes. *Total Quality Management (TQM)*: An organization-wide approach with 100% employee involvement, covering 100% processes with target of zero defects. and continuous quality improvement. *Failure Mode and Effects Analysis (FMEA)*: Identifies failure modes, causes, and prioritises failures with a priority score based on probability of occurrence, the severity of failure and its detectability. and mitigates potential failure points in processes. *Root Cause Analysis*: Identifies the underlying causes of defects or problems. *7 QC tools (which are quantitative)*: Check sheet, Graphs, Histogram, Scatter diagram, Fishbone diagram, Pareto graph, and Control charts.

7 QC Management tools (which are qualitative) namely affinity diagram,

Interrelationship Diagram, Prioritisation diagram, Matrix diagram, Matrix Data Analysis, Process decision program chart, Arrow diagram.

Quality Assurance vs. Quality Control
Quality Assurance (QA): Proactive measures to prevent defects by focusing on the process.
Quality Control (QC): Reactive measures to identify and correct defects in the final product.

Both QA and QC are essential for a comprehensive quality management strategy, with QA emphasizing prevention and QC focusing on detection and correction.

Six Sigma

The six sigma approach was first introduced and developed at Motorola in early 1990s. Credit for coining the term "Six Sigma," a federally registered trademark of Motorola, goes to a Motorola engineer named Bill Smith who worked under initiative of Bob Galvin, Chairman of Motorola. Later in the mid-nineties it was adopted by GE and Allied Signal. According to Jack Welch, ex CEO of GE, 'Six Sigma is the most challenging and potentially rewarding strategy GE has ever undertaken.'

Six Sigma quality level is 3.4 ppm (parts per million) or 99.9997% perfect. A 2% quality level, which was the acceptable quality level (AQL) in recent past, is 20000 ppm, and way away from the six sigma target for world class performance. Six sigma is customer focused, top driven business strategy, using process approach, facts and data and a statistical based quality metric.

Sigma is a Greek word used to describe variability. In statistical quality control, this means "standard deviation" (σ for population, and s for sampling distribution), which is a measure of dispersion around the mean.

$$s = \sqrt{\frac{\sum(x_i - \bar{x})^2}{n - 1}}$$

The six-sigma approach should be used when the answers to following three questions are as under:

1. Is there a problem or opportunity?...both
2. Is the cause of the problem known?...No
3. Is the solution obvious?..................No

Sigma level	DPMO	COQ as % of sales
2	308537	too high!
3	66807	25-40%
4	6210	15-25%
5	233	5-15%
6	3.4	less then 1%

DPMO-defect per million opportunities

COQ- Cost of Quality

The highest quality producer is also the lowest cost producer.

Six sigma follows the **DMAIC** approach to problem solving.

Define (D)

What is the business affecting problem?

Identify the customer, Prepare high level process map, Define scope of project, resource requirements, due date, and deliverables.

Measure (M)

What are the metrics? How is measurement done? Are measurements reliable? Is data available? How do we measure progress and success of the project?

Analyse (A)

Analyse process flow, define handoffs, develop and validate hypothesis, root cause analysis.

Improve (I)

Develop ideas to remove root cause, implement solutions, test results, standardise.

Control (C)

Document process, check points to control performance.

Tools for DMAIC

Define	Voice of customer, Brainstorming, SIPOC diagram (process map - S Supplier, I Input, P Process steps, O Output, C Customer), Benchmarking, Pareto diagram, Project tracking, Customer satisfaction survey.
Measure	Metrics and data sheet on yield, quality, breakdowns etc, Process capability indices Cp and Cpk, OEE (Overall equipment effectiveness), sigma level, mean and sigma, benchmarking.
Analyse	Distribution-mean, sigma, histogram, distribution graph; Pareto analysis, graphs, scatter diagram, check sheets, control charts, cause and effect or fish bone diagram, why..why and 6W2H analysis, root cause analysis, regression analysis, hypothesis testing, design of experiments, ANOVA.

Improve	Kaizen, technology, poka yoke, six thinking hats, lateral thinking, brainstorming.
Control	Statistical Process Control, Visual controls, project tracking, control sheets and check sheets.

For doing a successful six sigma project, the person leading the team must show leadership, positive mindset, good knowledge of advanced statistics, and must have good project management, and technical skills.

In six sigma, a technical problem is formulated as a statistical problem, for which statistical solution is found, which has to be then converted into a technical solution. For example, noise coming from car may be because of many variables. The statistical study will identify variables which are most significant contributors to the noise. It is then for the technical team to find solutions for elimination of the bad effects of identified variables.

27
Project Management

Project management is the application of knowledge, skills, tools, and techniques to project activities to meet project requirements.

Projects are temporary in nature while production is ongoing involving work that is continuous without an ending date and often repeats the same process. Projects have definitive start dates and definitive end dates. Project is completed when goals and objectives of project are accomplished.

Objectives

The objectives of project management are:

- To complete the project on time as per plan and within customer's requirements.
- To complete the project within cost as budgeted.
- To meet the performance, safety and quality standards as set for the project to meet customer specifications and satisfaction.
- To satisfy all stakeholders.

- To be ethical.

Project Management Phases

1. **Initiation** : Defining the project, its purpose, objectives, and scope.
2. **Planning** : Developing a detailed project plan including schedules, resources, and budget.
3. **Execution** : Implementing the project plan and carrying out project activities.
4. **Monitoring and Controlling** : Tracking project progress, identifying issues, and making necessary adjustments.
5. **Closing** : Finalising all project activities, handing over deliverables, and closing out the project.

Key Concepts in Project Management

Scope: The work required to complete the project.

Time: The schedule for completing the project.

Precedence: The tasks which must be completed before the next activity starts.

Cost: The budget allocated for the project.

Resource management : manpower, equipment, money; resource scheduling.

Quality: The standards and criteria the project must meet.

Risk: Potential issues that could affect the project's success.

Stakeholders: Individuals or groups with an interest in the project.

Scope Creep: Managing changes to the project scope through clear communication and change control processes.

Project Management Knowledge Areas

1. Project Integration Management
2. Project Scope Management
3. Project Time Management
4. Project Cost Management
5. Project Quality Management
6. Project Human Resource Management
7. Project Communications Management
8. Project Risk Management
9. Project Procurement Management

Project Planning Tools and Techniques

Work Breakdown Structure (WBS) : A hierarchical decomposition of the total scope of work.

Gantt Charts : Visual timelines for tasks.

PERT Charts : Project evaluation and review technique for analysing task dependencies and timelines.

Critical Path Method (CPM): Identifying the longest path of dependent activities to determine the project duration.

Project Execution and Control

Resource Allocation : Assigning and managing resources (people, equipment, materials) effectively.

Communication Management : Ensuring timely and effective communication among stakeholders.

Performance Metrics: Tracking key performance indicators (KPIs) such as on-time completion, budget adherence, and quality standards.

Risk Management

Risk Identification : Recognizing potential risks that could impact the project.

Risk Assessment : Evaluating the likelihood and impact of identified risks.

Risk Mitigation : Developing strategies to minimize or manage risks.

Project Charter

Project Charter should include:

- An overview of the project
- Project goals
- Project deliverables
- Business case or need for the project
- Product description
- Resource and cost estimates
- Feasibility study results
- Human resources and skills required
- Roles and responsibilities of key team members and resources
- List of key stakeholders
- Name of Project Manager, Project Sponsor, Project Champion, Functional Managers, Project Team

Project charter sign off

Between project sponsor, project manager and the senior management, and key stakeholders

Project Management Software

Microsoft Project : Comprehensive project management software for planning, tracking, and reporting.

Primavera : Advanced project management software for large-scale projects.

The Project Life Cycle

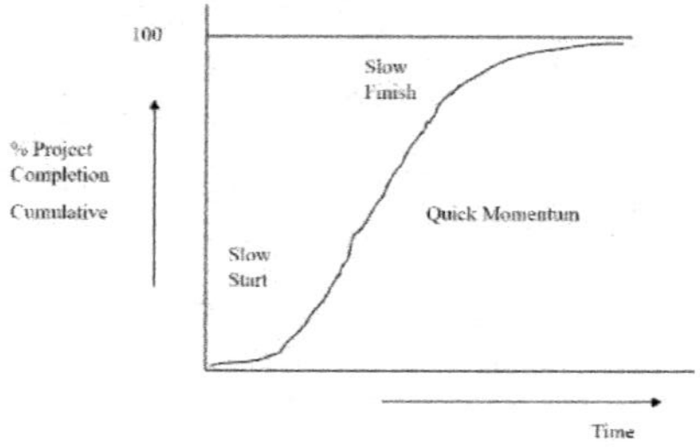
100
% Project
Completion
Cumulative
Slow
Start
Slow
Finish
Quick Momentum
Time

J.M.Pant
Management Consultant, Trainer and Visiting Professor
+919811030273, jm.pant@gmail.com

The Project Life Cycle

- Time Distribution

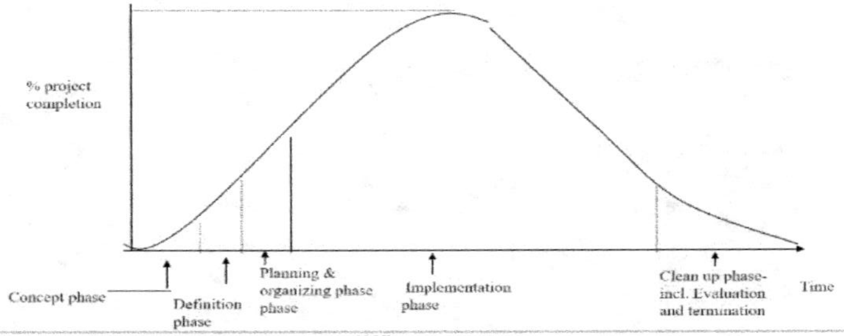
% project completion
Concept phase
Definition phase
Planning & organizing phase phase
Implementation phase
Clean up phase- incl. Evaluation and termination
Time

J.M.Pant
Management Consultant, Trainer and Visiting Professor
+919811030273, jm.pant@gmail.com

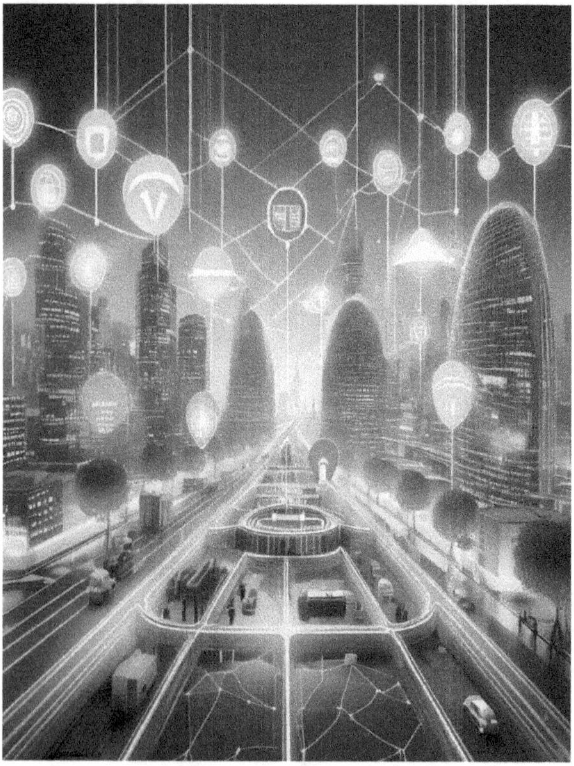

28
IoT in Operations Management

The Internet of Things (IoT) is the interconnected network of physical devices embedded with sensors, software, and other technologies to exchange data with other devices and systems over the internet. This connectivity allows for real-time data collection, analysis, and action, significantly enhancing operations management across various industries.

IoT Components

1. ***Sensors and Actuators***

Sensors collect data from the environment, such as temperature, humidity, motion, and pressure. Actuators, on the other hand, perform actions based on the processed data, such as adjusting a valve or turning on a light.

2. ***Connectivity***

Devices communicate through various means, including Wi-Fi, Bluetooth, cellular networks, and low-power wide-area networks (LPWANs). Reliable connectivity is crucial for real-time data transmission.

3. *Data Processing*

Edge computing processes data locally on the device or nearby, reducing latency and bandwidth use. Cloud computing offers extensive storage and powerful analytics capabilities for large-scale data processing.

4. *User Interface*

Dashboards and mobile apps provide a user-friendly interface to monitor and control IoT devices, enabling easy access to data and system management.

Applications of IoT in Operations Management

1. Predictive Maintenance

<Example>: In a manufacturing plant, IoT sensors on machinery monitor vibration, temperature, and other performance indicators. Advanced analytics predict when a machine is likely to fail, allowing maintenance to be scheduled before a breakdown occurs. This reduces downtime and maintenance costs.

2. Inventory Management

<Example>: IoT-enabled RFID tags and smart shelves track inventory levels in real-time. When stock levels drop below a certain threshold, the system automatically places an order, ensuring optimal inventory levels and reducing the risk of stockouts.

3. Supply Chain Optimisation

<Example> : IoT devices monitor the location and condition of goods in transit. For instance, temperature sensors in refrigerated trucks ensure perishable goods are kept within the required temperature range. Real-time tracking helps in route optimisation and enhances supply chain transparency.

4. Energy Management

<Example> : Smart meters and sensors monitor energy usage in a facility. The data collected helps identify energy wastage and optimise consumption. Automated systems can adjust lighting, heating, and cooling based on occupancy and environmental conditions, reducing energy costs.

5. Quality Control

<Example> : In food processing, IoT sensors monitor critical parameters such as temperature and humidity throughout the production process. Data analytics detect any deviations from quality standards in real-time, ensuring high-quality output and reducing waste.

29
Role of IT and Data Analytics in Operations Management

Information Technology (IT) has become an integral component of operations management, transforming the way businesses operate and compete. Its influence spans across various aspects of operations, enhancing efficiency, accuracy, and decision-making capabilities.

1.Process Automation in Manufacturing and Production, Service Operations

IT enables automation of manufacturing processes through the use of robotics, computer-aided design (CAD), and computer-aided manufacturing (CAM) systems. This leads to increased precision, reduced labour costs, and higher production speeds. In service industries, IT supports automation through customer relationship management (CRM) systems, automated call centers, and self-service kiosks, improving customer experience and operational efficiency.

2. Data Management and Analytics

IT systems facilitate real-time data collection from various operational processes, providing immediate insights into performance and efficiency. Advanced analytics tools process large volumes of data to identify trends, predict demand, and optimise supply chains, enhancing decision-making and strategic planning.

3. Supply Chain Management (SCM) IT enables the integration of supply chain components through Enterprise Resource Planning (ERP) systems, which provide a unified view of operations from customer acquisition, material procurement, production to shipment back to customer. ***Tracking and Traceability***: Technologies such as RFID (Radio Frequency Identification) and GPS (Global Positioning System) enhance the tracking and traceability of goods, improving inventory management and reducing losses including due to pilferage and theft.

4. Quality Control and Improvement

Automated Quality Inspections: IT facilitates automated inspection systems using machine vision and sensors to detect defects and ensure quality standards. ***Statistical Process Control***: Software tools for statistical process control (SPC) help monitor and control production processes through control charts, reducing variability and enhancing product quality aiming at zero defects.

5. Customer Relationship Management (CRM)

IT supports CRM, which helps manage interactions, track customer preferences, and personalise services, by integrating customer data across various touchpoints. The customer feedback and engagement becomes continuous and online, fostering loyalty, stronger customer relationships and continuous improvement.

6. Enterprise Resource Planning (ERP)

Enterprise Resource Planning (ERP) systems are comprehensive software platforms which streamline, optimise and integrate various business processes, including sales, marketing, production, procurement, stores, quality, finance, HR, and supply chain management, providing a holistic view and improving resource allocation, efficiency, productivity, and decision-making.

Consider a mid-sized manufacturing company that struggles with disparate systems for production planning, scheduling and control, inventory, finance, sales, and human resources. By implementing an ERP system, the company can integrate these functions into a single platform. Inventory levels are updated in real-time, production schedules as per demand, financial reports are generated automatically, and HR processes like payroll and employee management are streamlined..

7.Others

Advanced algorithms and optimisation tools help in scheduling, routing, and resource allocation, ensuring optimal use of resources..

Collaboration Platforms: IT facilitates enhanced communication and collaboration through platforms like Google Meet, Microsoft Teams, and Zoom. These tools support real-time communication, file sharing, presentations and project management. ***Cloud Computing***: Cloud-based solutions provide scalable resources and enable remote access to operational data and applications. ***Security and Risk Management.*** IT plays a crucial role in safeguarding operational data through cybersecurity measures such as block chain, encryption, firewalls, and intrusion detection systems. They help identify and mitigate risks by monitoring operations, detecting anomalies, and providing contingency planning tools. ***Sustainability and Environmental Impact*** IT supports sustainability initiatives through energy management systems that monitor and optimise energy usage, reducing environmental impact. IT enables the implementation of sustainable practices by tracking resource usage, waste management, and compliance with environmental regulations.

30
Mechatronics, Automation

Mechatronics and automation are pivotal fields in modern engineering, driving innovation across industries, promoting efficiency, quality and cost savings, safety and flexibility. They combine mechanical engineering, electronics, computer science, and control engineering to create smarter, intelligent systems and automated processes. From manufacturing to healthcare, these disciplines are revolutionising how we design, produce, and interact with technology.

Mechatronics

The key components of mechatronics are the physical structure and moving parts, electronic systems like sensors, actuators, and microcontrollers that process signals and control mechanical systems. The control systems, software and hardware integration comprise of algorithms and feedback mechanisms that manage the operation of the mechanical and electronic components.

The applications of Mechatronics includes Robotics which is designing robots for manufacturing, medical surgery, exploration, and household tasks; Automotive Systems; Consumer Electronics like smartphones, cameras, and other appliances.

Automation involves using control systems, such as computers and robots, to operate machinery and processes with minimal human intervention. It aims to increase efficiency, accuracy, and productivity while reducing costs and human error. Applications of Automation are in ①Manufacturing - Enhancing production lines, quality control, and packaging processes; ②Logistics comprise of Automating warehousing, inventory management, and transportation systems, ③Agriculture includes implementing automated irrigation, harvesting, and sorting and grading systems; ④ Healthcare utilising automation in diagnostics, laboratory testing, and patient monitoring.

Types of Automation

1. Fixed Automation: Using specialized equipment for mass production. Examples include assembly lines and stamping machines.
2. Programmable Automation: Allows for changes in the operation sequence to produce different products. Examples include CNC machines and programmable logic controllers (PLCs).
3. Flexible Automation: Enables the production of a variety of products with minimal changeover time. Examples include robotic arms and automated guided vehicles (AGVs).

Automated Manufacturing Systems comprises of mechanical components like conveyors, robotic arms, and assembly machines; electronic components includes sensors and actuators for precise control and feedback; control systems namely PLCs and microcontrollers to manage and coordinate the processes and software for monitoring, data analysis, and optimisation.

Artificial Intelligence (AI) and Machine Learning (ML) enhance automation with intelligent decision-making and predictive maintenance.

Internet of Things (IoT) connect devices for real-time data sharing and monitoring.

Collaborative Robots (Cobots), that is, Robots working alongside humans, enhancing productivity and safety.

Advanced Sensing and Vision Systems improve precision and adaptability in automation.

The benefits of automation are several and the challenge is the large investment and high initial costs, skilled workforce, and complexity.

.

31
Green Technology and Environment Sustainability

The integration of green technology and environmental considerations into operations management is increasingly crucial for achieving sustainable business practices.

Green Technology

Green technology refers to the use of environmentally friendly practices and innovations to reduce the negative impact of operations on the environment. Incorporating green technology into operations management helps businesses meet regulatory requirements, reduce costs, and improve their corporate image.

Sustainable Operations Management Practices

- ***Energy Efficiency***: Implementing energy-efficient technologies and practices, such as LED lighting, energy-efficient HVAC systems, and equipment with low power consumption,

reduces energy use and operational costs.
- ***Waste Reduction***: Adopting waste reduction techniques like lean manufacturing, recycling programs, and waste-to-energy technologies minimises waste generation and disposal costs.
- ***Water Conservation***: Implementing water-saving technologies, such as low-flow fixtures and sensors for on-off of water supply, water recycling systems, rain harvesting, check dams, and smart drip irrigation, helps conserve water and reduce utility expenses.

Green Supply Chain Management

- ***Sustainable Sourcing***: Choosing suppliers that adhere to environmental standards and use sustainable practices ensures that the entire supply chain supports environmental goals.
- ***Eco-Friendly Transportation***: Utilising fuel-efficient vehicles (like Electric Vehicles), optimising routes, and adopting alternative fuel sources like electric and hybrid vehicles reduce the carbon footprint of transportation activities.
- ***Green Packaging***: Implementing packaging solutions that use recyclable or biodegradable materials, reduce packaging waste, and

minimise resource consumption.

Renewable Energy Integration

- ***Solar Power***: Installing solar panels on production facilities and office buildings to generate renewable energy reduces reliance on fossil fuels and lowers greenhouse gas emissions.
- ***Wind Energy***: Utilising wind turbines to generate electricity for operations, particularly in areas with high wind potential, contributes to a sustainable energy mix.
- ***Energy Storage***: Implementing energy storage solutions, such as batteries, to store excess renewable energy for use during peak demand periods or when not generating.
-***Other sources of energy***. Biomass like sugar bagasse, rice husk; tidal energy; geothermal energy.

Sustainable Product Design and Lifecycle Management

- ***Eco-Design Principles***: Incorporating eco-design principles into product development to minimise environmental impact throughout

the product lifecycle, including material selection, bio degradable items, manufacturing processes, and end-of-life disposal.
- ***Lifecycle Assessment (LCA)***: Conducting LCAs to evaluate the environmental impact of products from cradle to grave and identify opportunities for improvement.

Environmental Management Systems (EMS)

- **ISO 14001 Certification**: Implementing an Environmental Management System (EMS) based on ISO 14001 standards to systematically manage environmental responsibilities and improve overall environmental performance through Continuous Improvement using the Plan-Do-Check-Act (PDCA) cycle to monitor, review, and improve environmental performance and compliance with environmental regulations.

Green Information Technology (Green IT)

- Energy-Efficient Data Centers: Designing data centers with energy-efficient cooling systems, virtualisation, and server

consolidation to reduce energy consumption.
- E-Waste Management: Implementing e-waste recycling programs and ensuring proper disposal of electronic devices to minimize environmental impact.

Green Hydrogen and Green Steel Making: Paving the Way to a Sustainable Future

Two emerging technologies—green hydrogen and green steel making—are gaining attention for their potential to revolutionise industries traditionally associated with high carbon emissions.

Green Hydrogen: The Clean Fuel of the Future

Green hydrogen is hydrogen produced through the process of electrolysis powered by renewable energy sources such as wind, solar, or hydroelectric power. Unlike conventional hydrogen, which is produced from natural gas and emits significant CO_2, or "blue" hydrogen, which captures and stores emissions, green hydrogen generates no greenhouse gases during production.

Green Steel Making: Reducing Carbon Footprints in Heavy Industry. Green steel is steel produced using methods that significantly reduce carbon emissions compared to traditional steel making processes. The traditional blast furnace method relies heavily on coal, a major source of CO_2 emissions. In contrast, green steel production uses alternative methods, including the use of green hydrogen.

Integrating green technology and environmental considerations into operations management is essential for building sustainable and resilient businesses. By adopting energy-efficient practices, sustainable sourcing, renewable energy, and environmentally friendly technologies, organisations can reduce their environmental impact, achieve regulatory compliance, and enhance their competitiveness. Embracing sustainability in operations not only benefits the environment but also drives differentiation in global market, long-term profitability and growth.

32
AI and Machine Learning

Artificial Intelligence (AI) and Machine Learning (ML) are transformative technologies that are reshaping operations management across industries. AI involves creating systems capable of performing tasks that normally require human intelligence, such as decision-making, pattern recognition, and language understanding. ML, a subset of AI, focuses on developing algorithms that allow systems to learn from and make predictions based on data.

The benefits in Operations Management are ① higher efficiency as AI and ML automate routine tasks and optimise processes, ② enhanced decision-Making through data-driven insights from AI and ML models, ③ cost savings, ④ increased agility as AI-powered systems enable businesses to respond quickly to market changes and customer demands.⑤ better quality.

The challenges of implementing AI and ML are data quality and availability; integration with existing systems requiring investment in technology and skills; ethical, legal and regulatory considerations of data privacy, security, and ethical use of AI and ML; and scarcity of talented professionals skilled in AI and ML.

Key Concepts in AI and ML

1. **Artificial Intelligence (AI)**

AI refers to the simulation of human intelligence in machines. It encompasses a range of technologies, including:

- ***Natural Language Processing (NLP)***: Enabling machines to understand and respond to human language.
- ***Computer Vision***: Allowing machines to interpret and make decisions based on visual inputs.
- ***Expert Systems***: Utilising knowledge and inference rules to simulate human decision-making.

2. ***Machine Learning*** (ML)

ML is a branch of AI that focuses on building algorithms that can learn from and make decisions based on data. Key types include:

- ***Supervised Learning***: Algorithms are trained on labelled data, meaning the input comes with the correct output.
- ***Unsupervised Learning***: Algorithms find patterns in unlabelled data without predefined outcomes.
-***Reinforcement Learning***: Algorithms learn by interacting with an environment to maximise some notion of cumulative reward.

Applications of AI and ML in Operations Management

1. ***Predictive Maintenance***
<Example>: Manufacturing plants use ML algorithms to predict equipment failures before they occur. By analysing historical data on machine performance and maintenance records, these systems can forecast when a machine is likely to fail and schedule maintenance accordingly. This reduces downtime and maintenance costs.

2. Inventory Management
<Example>: Retailers utilise AI to optimize inventory levels. ML models analyse sales data, seasonal trends, and customer behaviour to

predict future demand. This helps maintain optimal inventory levels, reducing the costs associated with overstocking and stockouts.

3. ***Supply Chain Optimisation***

<Example>: AI-driven supply chain management systems can forecast demand, optimise logistics, and manage supplier relationships. For instance, ML algorithms can analyse traffic patterns and weather conditions to suggest the most efficient delivery routes, reducing transportation costs and improving delivery times.

4. Quality Control

<Example>: In the automotive industry, computer vision systems powered by AI inspect parts and assemblies on production lines. These systems can detect defects with greater accuracy and speed than human inspectors, ensuring higher quality products and reducing waste.

5. Demand Forecasting

<Example>: E-commerce platforms use AI to predict customer demand. By analysing data from various sources, such as social media,

economic indicators, and historical sales, AI models can provide accurate demand forecasts, helping businesses plan production and inventory more effectively.

Future Trends

1. **AI-Driven Automation**: The integration of AI with robotic process automation (RPA) will further streamline operations, reducing the need for human intervention in repetitive tasks.
2. **Edge AI** : Processing data closer to where it is generated (at the edge) will reduce latency and enable real-time decision-making in applications such as autonomous vehicles and smart factories.
3. **Explainable AI (XAI)** : As AI systems become more complex, there will be a greater focus on making AI decisions transparent and understandable to build trust and ensure accountability.
4. **AI-Enhanced Human-Machine Collaboration** : AI will augment human capabilities, enabling more effective collaboration between workers and intelligent systems.

Scenario: The AI-Enhanced Warehouse.

Imagine a large e-commerce company's warehouse where AI and ML are fully integrated. Autonomous robots, guided by ML algorithms, navigate the warehouse, picking and packing orders with incredible efficiency. Sensors and IoT devices monitor the condition of the robots and the environment, feeding data into an AI system that predicts maintenance needs and optimises operations. Employees oversee the process through an intuitive dashboard, making data-driven decisions to improve workflow. This AI-enhanced warehouse operates at peak efficiency, ensuring fast, accurate order fulfilment and a seamless customer experience.

33
The Journey Ahead

The discipline of Operations Management is vast, and the book's limited purpose is to whet the reader's appetite to delve into the field of Operations and learn more through on the job experience supported by reading resources. I did not realise till I finished writing that the teaser itself has become 300 pages!

Throughout this book, I have explored the multifaceted domain of Operations Management, touching key areas that form the backbone of effective business operations. The goals of Operations Management are to improve Quality, Productivity, Safety, Delivery, Morale and reduce Cost using relevant tools and techniques of plant layout, industrial engineering, PPC and SCM, JIT and Kanban, Kaizen, 5S, Six sigma, reducing and eliminating wastes covered comprehensively under Muda, Mura and Muri, and many more.

Operations Management has undergone substantial evolution, driven by technological advancements and changing market dynamics.

The transition from manual processes to automated systems, robotics, data analytics and integration through ERP (Enterprise Resource Planning) has revolutionised manufacturing and service industries alike. Technological innovation, from early mechanisation to contemporary digital transformation with AI and ML, has continually reshaped the landscape of efficiency and precision.

Practice on the job, in shop floor and your work place or work station, explore, discover and read more to stay abreast, motivated and updated in this wonderful world of Operations Management, a dynamic and ever-evolving field that plays a crucial role in the success of business organisations.

Training employees of Adani Agrifresh, Himachal Pradesh (apple warehousing)-

At Tehri Dam, program on TQM with THDC

Jitendra.M.Pant

Mentor, Life Coach, and Trainer
Inspirational Founder of JMPS Health & Education Care Foundation

Jitendra .M. Pant is a seasoned and distinguished mentor, life coach, and trainer, specialising in personal and professional transformation, with a versatile skill set honed through extensive experience in Operations Management. An avid lifelong learner and with a rich background encompassing over 45 years of non-linear career growth, he has been deeply engaged in various sectors of manufacturing industry, services, consultancy and education.

Apart from his professional endeavours, Jitendra.M.Pant is a creative author and storyteller, weaving captivating tales in prose and verse which have the stamp of his personal journey, sharp observations of industry, work units and a unique blend of practical expertise and creative expression. He motivates individuals to achieve excellence, exude confidence and resolve problems, in his mentoring sessions supported with his self-help books.

In October 2023, in his senior citizen years, driven by a spirit of service and altruism and an overwhelming desire to do something for others in need, Jitendra.M.Pant founded the JMPS Health & Education Care Foundation, registered as a section 8 company. This NGO is committed to making a meaningful impact in health and education sectors.

His diverse skill set, interdisciplinary experience, and a solid foundation in technical education and learning are exemplified by his academic journey, having earned both B. Tech and M. Tech degrees from the prestigious IIT Delhi.

Following books have been written by J.M.Pant :

1. **5S: First Vital Step Towards Operations Excellence (A5 page size)-**A Practice Oriented Book for 5S Awareness & Implementation.
2. **5S: Foundation for Operations & Personal Excellence-** A Practice Oriented Text With Online and Site support.
3. **Time Management** -For higher personal productivity.
4. **25 Lessons from uncommon thoughts**
5. **Problem Solving**
   Simple tools and techniques which everyone can understand
6. **Confidence Building**
   For personal happiness
7. **No**
   Say No, Be Happy
8. **Wisdom in Verses**
   A Grandfather's Reflection
9. **Nano Insights**
   Everyday Observations Sparking Micro Stories

Books available online on pothi.com, amazon.in and flipkart.com

Website of NGO
www.jmpshealthedu.co.in

www.ingramcontent.com/pod-product-compliance
Lightning Source LLC
Chambersburg PA
CBHW071911210526
45479CB00002B/375
9798333757654